*Mary's
Message of
Hope*

VOLUME TWO

Other books by Annie and Byron Kirkwood

*Mary's Message to the World* (Annie Kirkwood)
*Messages to Our Family* (Annie & Byron Kirkwood)
*Instructions for the Soul* (Annie & Byron)
*Mary's Message of Hope, Vol. 1* (Annie)
*Mary's Message of Love* (Annie)
*Survival Guide for the New Millennium* (Byron Kirkwood)

# Mary's Message of Hope

## VOLUME TWO

*As Sent by Mary,
the Mother of Jesus,
to Her Messenger*

Annie Kirkwood

BLUE DOLPHIN

Copyright © 2002 Annie Kirkwood
All rights reserved.

Published by Blue Dolphin Publishing, Inc.
P.O. Box 8, Nevada City, CA 95959
Orders: 1-800-643-0765
Web: www.bluedolphinpublishing.com

ISBN: 1-57733-062-5

Library of Congress Cataloging-in-Publication Data

Mary, Blessed Virgin, Saint (Spirit)
   Mary's message of hope / as sent by Mary the mother of Jesus to her messenger Annie Kirkwood.
     p.   cm.
   ISBN 1-57733-062-5
   1. Spirit writings. 2. Spiritual life. I. Kirkwood, Annie, 1937– . II. Title.
BF1301.M36 1995
133.9'3—dc20                                           95-42600
                                                                  CIP

First printing: May 2002

Cover painting by Tamara Berault
Cover design by Jeff Case

Printed in the United States of America

10   9   8   7   6   5   4   3   2   1

*Dedication*

This book is dedicated to
and all the readers of
*Mary's Message Newsletter*

# Table of Contents

|    | Introduction | ix |
|----|---|---|
| 31 | Peace Is a Way of Life | 149 |
| 32 | Keep the Faith | 155 |
| 33 | Faith Creates Your Future | 161 |
| 34 | You Can Make a Difference | 168 |
| 35 | The Real Gift | 175 |
| 36 | Live in Peace | 182 |
| 37 | Peace Is Serenity | 188 |
| 38 | Be Faithful in Your Prayers | 195 |
| 39 | Seek God's Solace | 202 |
| 40 | Each Day Is a Gift | 209 |
| 41 | Live in Joy | 216 |
| 42 | Be Grateful for Your Blessings | 223 |
| 43 | Promote Peace | 230 |
| 44 | True Peace Is Alive | 237 |
| 45 | Pray for Peace | 244 |
| 46 | Conclave for Peace | 251 |

| 47 | Increase Your Faith | 258 |
| 48 | Prayer Brings Change | 265 |
| 49 | The Birth of Christ | 273 |
| 50 | A Time of Change | 279 |
| 51 | The Power of Resurrection | 286 |
| 52 | Truth Clears the Way | 293 |
| 53 | Serenity | 300 |
| 54 | Hold on to Hope | 307 |

# *Introduction*

IT HAS BEEN A SOURCE OF AMAZEMENT that these messages keep coming. I thought when I'd finished receiving the messages that became *Mary's Message to the World,* I was finished. And except for personal messages, this seemed to be the case. Then in 1992, Mother Mary asked us to send "Her messages" to you, "Her readers." These were first sent out as a newsletter, originally by mail and now also on our website. Since then I've been expecting them to stop at any time. Periodically I will ask, "Am I through, or will the messages continue?" As you can see, it continues, and every other month I receive a new message.

Over the years Mother Mary has urged me to live her message. In my section of the newsletter I write about my experiences. She also urges me to be honest about what and how I am living this message. It has not always been an easy thing to do. But six times a year I feel like I bare my soul. Thank God, I've come to believe that the newsletter subscribers are my friends; it makes it easier.

I've met many of you across the nation as I've traveled. I've talked to you on the phone, and many of you write to let me know that you too are trying to live the message. Often you've let me know that we share experiences, or that you too are experiencing similar events or situations in your life. Now in book form, these same messages take on a new life, because many more people are reached. As you will read, I cry, get angry, love, doubt, am filled with joy, and feel the darkest despair from time to time. In my very human life I am trying to live a God-filled life, one that is filled with peace, joy, and unconditional love.

Needless to say, Mother Mary's messages are always awe-inspiring. There is nothing to explain except to say it has been a blessing beyond imagination to have been chosen as Her messenger. She is always loving, patient, compassionate, serene, and encouraging. Mother Mary inspires, enfolds one with Her deep love, and explains how to have hope, peace, and love in our lives. As is often said to me, "You can live the message. It's simple, but not easy."

I hope you derive a similar inspiration to change your life. From experience I can tell you that, because I have lived her message to the best of my ability, I have changed dramatically, been healed of a deep-seated anger, and been able to forgive those responsible for childhood sexual abuse. A note, my father was not one of my abusers and for that I am grateful. I encourage you to take to heart Mother Mary's words and let them make a difference in your life, like they have in mine. You will become more peaceful, understanding, tolerant, and loving as I have, and it feels good.

Annie Kirkwood

# 31

## Peace Is a Way of Life

12/96

FOR THOSE WHO ARE NEW TO THE NEWSLETTER, several years ago, at the suggestion of The Brotherhood, we began to write letters of appreciation to each other at Christmas. We remember the special things they did to help us, the meaning that the person has given to our lives, the many ways they have impacted our lives, and we let them know how much we love and appreciate them.

Sometimes a family member doesn't have to do anything to impact our lives. For instance we have a son, Mark, who has Down's Syndrome. All he has to do is . . . be. By being himself, he brings an added depth to our lives that we would otherwise miss. So we appreciate deeds, words, but most of all we appreciate our family for simply being our family, and for being themselves.

I've been asked about family members who remain estranged, or whom we still haven't been able to forgive, or perhaps to forget past hurts they inflicted. Sometimes a printed Christmas card is all that is needed. Or perhaps a Christmas card with a handwritten note that says I'm remembering past Christmases. We can always remember a happy time during the holidays. Christmas is a good time to open doors for peace to enter. We can let people know that our feelings have changed. I was reminding myself that Mother Mary says we chose our family of origin. What I've learned is that *our first family, the one we are born into and/or the one who raised us, if we are adopted, was chosen to help us work out some karmic residue. So if your choice is a family with problems, remind yourself . . . this is your choice. You thought this was the best place, family, and time to work out or finish something from the past. You don't have to remember the past life; all you have to do is heal the hurts, the issues that your family of origin bring you. As I was thinking about why I had chosen particular family members, Mother Mary said, "The greatest gift one soul can give another is to come into your life to be your nemesis." This one statement gives a whole new meaning to problem people in your life. It's also given me a whole new perspective on family members who abused or misused me. I realize that the only thing that is real is . . . love.*

*When you begin to open the door to estranged family members, remember that just because you've changed, doesn't mean they have. I recall when I began to change within and felt more understanding and loving towards family I'd been estranged from. My expectation was that since I'd changed and felt warm towards them, that they would feel the same. But it doesn't always work that way. You can honor and respect their position and maintain your willingness for a new relationship. We can't be all things to all people. There are times we disappoint or disillusion others. This is inevitable if they have not taken the time to really get to know you and how you think or feel. More often it's that they have certain expectations of you that are not in keeping with who you are. At times we must distance ourselves from family and/or friends in order to have peace of mind. This doesn't mean we are bad or unloving. It means we love ourselves enough to take care of ourselves. It means we honor and respect ourselves and tend to our needs. We are the only one who can take care of our needs. We are the only one who can make our choices. We can let people know that we are thinking of them, even if we don't always agree. So if you have family or friends who come to mind during this season, let them know you are thinking of them. Sometimes that is all that is needed.*

*I appreciate each of you. You are friends who are also seeking to have a close connection to God. Many of you have sent cards, thoughts, and prayers during this year. In February I fell and broke my leg. Your prayers for my health have worked wonders and I've felt your support. You have given me a year of love. I recognize it and appreciate it.*

*But most of all I appreciate our Creator for His goodness and love in my life. I appreciate my family. And I appreciate the work He has given me to do. I appreciate Mother Mary and The Brotherhood. I am truly blessed. —annie*

◇ ◇ ◇

My Dear Children, it is with great joy that I come today. I remind you of the peace which surrounds this world and which is simply waiting for a place within your heart. Peace, Love, Light and all of God's Goodness are already here waiting for a place within your mind and heart in which to live. God can only work through you. You are responsible for setting up a welcoming place within your heart. Peace will not come to the heart filled with hatred, resentments, jealousy, and selfishness. Peace will only reside in a heart that is working towards forgiveness, and loving unselfishly and unconditionally. You do not have to have forgiven everything; as you forgive, as you love . . . peace grows within you. It fills voids that you hadn't recognized. It overflows into places that you thought were lost. It shines in the darkest corners of your heart once you have made up your mind to live in peace. It takes perseverance, commitment, and the desire to have peace in your heart, mind, and life. Once this great decision is made, you will find that the things that need to be eliminated will bring you the gift of forgiveness. They bring you opportunities to live in peace. One prayer is all it takes when it comes from the heart and with full mental agreement. Do not get overtaken by the commercialism of this season. Give gifts that come from your heart and give them every day. Celebrate the season of peace every day of the year. Then peace will surely come to earth.

During this season of the year, as I see many people become concerned with others, I urge you to stay concerned with others every day of the year. I see people making great plans for family, but not all families are making plans for every member of the family. Love your family unconditionally. Put aside your own personal judgments concerning others. Do not concentrate on how they should live, or how they dress, nor on who they are with, nor on any other facet of your family members' lives. Your whole purpose in life is to love unconditionally as you love yourself, and as you love God. Include every member of your family in your prayers, good thoughts, and in your love. Even those who have in the past harmed you in any way—each member of your family brings to you a great gift. It is the gift of healing, love, and peace.

Peace, my little children, is a way of life. Peace is not a destination. If you think that, when something occurs, or someone else changes, there will be peace, you will be disappointed. Peace will come to you when you determine to live in peace. Then when the decision is made, all that is keeping you from peace will enter your awareness. But this doesn't mean you failed; it simply means that you have succeeded. You cannot live in peace with disturbances of the heart or mind. So after you decide to live in peace, watch for the things that are keeping you from peace. Settle the issues of your life, heal the wounds, find ways to negotiate peace inside of your heart and mind.

Respect, acknowledge, and love each person who is in your life. Family is more than your blood relatives; family is the whole of mankind. Only when a good number of people begin to think of their family as the family of mankind, will people accept that every person is important to God. The people in your life, your friends, co-workers, acquaintances, and neighbors are here to give you a multitude of opportunities to love and be at peace. A thread runs through every person on earth and that thread is the love of God. Every person has within their being a unique and beautiful pattern. This pattern is their connection to God, to their own creativity and to their talents. This pattern is what makes each person different from others. No two people are alike. They may look alike on the outside, as in the case of twins, triplets, or siblings, but on the inside they will have a different way to express their creativity, and talents, and personality.

Love the differences; cease the urge to make everyone in your image. We are all created in God's image, and this is what makes each person wonderful. There is peace when you can accept the uniqueness and differences in people. There is peace when you can accept your own differences and appreciate your very own beautiful pattern. Being at peace means that you love unconditionally. Living in peace is living in vigilance. You are vigilant and aware of the circumstances and situations in your life. You can remove yourself gently from conflict when appropriate, and can be gentle and firm in how you treat yourself and others. Living in peace doesn't mean you become a doormat and allow others to misuse you or mistreat you. It means you love and respect yourself and the other person enough to remove the obstacles. You are honest with yourself at all times and can truly see the whole situation. If you react to a situation in your family because of what one person has said, you are not being honest. Look at every person, situation, and circumstance in your life in honesty and love.

You can do this, my children. If you pray for the eyes to see in truth . . . the ears to hear the truth . . . the understanding to decide in truth . . . you can live in peace. As one more person commits to live in peace, more peace is brought to earth through you. It takes a host of prayers, a legion of love, and one person at a time to bring peace to earth in your lifetime. Nothing is impossible to God. He will continue to whisper lovingly until you listen to His silent voice. He will guide you in all things. He will teach you how to live in peace when you seek His Truth.

Help me pray for your world. Help me pray for your family of mankind and above all pray for yourself. You are loved more than you know. You are more talented than you can imagine, and you have more abilities than you can realize. Peace on earth is possible when you allow God to work through you to create His peace in your life. I am loving you.

Mary, Mother of Jesus.

# 32

## Keep the Faith

2/97

SERENITY HAS BEEN MY GOAL *and also my measuring stick for some time. I've used the "Prayer of Serenity" not only as a prayer but as my measuring stick to let me know when I've stepped out of peace, or when future plans may take me into some situation that is potentially chaotic. When I used to be a drama queen, it was difficult to know beforehand if I was facing something that could upset me. Today I live for the most part in peace. When I become upset, I now recognize that I am out of my peaceful state. This is a big step forward for me, because for so many years I didn't realize I was upset until I was raging. When I realize that I'm not at peace now . . . I ask myself, "What can I do to get back to Peace and Serenity?"*

*We are like everyone else, having a human experience, at times forgetting that we are really spiritual beings in these bodies. I can get caught up in old patterns and find myself out of peace. Just last week, Byron was enjoying himself. He is a tease and loves to tease me. I was all right when I went in to take a nap, but I wasn't when I awoke. He teased, not knowing that something within me had changed, and I was completely out of peace. There is no longer the loud expression of anger, but I did pout. I pouted the whole next day. In the morning I was already forgiving everyone associated with my upset. I knew I had been the one who had caused it. But it felt so good to pout, I decided to take the day to enjoy the good pout*

*I had going. It wasn't hurting anyone and I knew that as soon as Byron returned to our home from his office, (which is 120 feet away from the house), I was going to make up with him. My form of pouting is being extremely quiet, to the point of being rude.*

*I took the day to really work with this idea of being and living in peace. What I found was that I was angrier with myself than with anyone else. There is an old adage in Spanish that says, if a person gets angry, he has two chores, or two jobs. First he gets angry, then he must become content again. This was certainly true of me. I had gotten out of peace, whether it was deliberate or not, and then it was totally up to me to return to peace.*

*One of the first things I reminded myself of is my commitment to live Mother Mary's message. I'm learning to love unconditionally all the time. Most of the time I do fairly well. But there are times, generally, when I'm not at peace, that I forget and fall back into old habits of judging myself and others harshly. I remind myself how good it feels to love unconditionally. I think this is true because I'm relieved of having to make decisions about people. When you love unconditionally it isn't your responsibility to grade your loved ones or to keep up with how they are doing. In recovery language it's called taking another person's inventory. When you love unconditionally, you're only responsible for your own inventory or inner work. This leaves me free to live in peace as long as I can forgive. Forgiveness is the best and easiest way to get back into a state of peace. I forgave myself for becoming upset, and I forgave Byron for taking offense at my upset, and I forgave everyone else who was involved, no matter how trivial their participation was.*

*We can live in peace every day. It takes work on our part; it takes us becoming aware the instant we are out of peace, and it takes our wanting to return to peace. But most of all, it takes love . . . unconditional, non-judging, and continuously giving. See, I can remember when I used to withhold my love to punish a loved one. Isn't it amazing the things we do to our loved ones, in the name of love? But now I know that unconditional love flows freely; it's never withheld for any reason. That doesn't mean I don't get angry or upset. It means I don't forget my primary objective: to love without judging, to live filled with inner peace all day, and to forgive myself and others as soon as I recognize the need for forgiveness. Believe me, it gets easier with practice.*

*This way of life really leaves us free to enjoy life, to live comfortably and to have fun. It has opened me up to using my sense of humor in good ways. I used to use my sense of humor to put down, to discount, and to be the first to point out my own failures. But now I find that we can have a sense of humor without the put-downs, or pointing the finger at errors. I thank my mate and partner for teaching me this very important lesson. Byron has a wonderful sense of humor and for this reason our marriage and life together is fun and enjoyable. I thank God for him.*

*So take it easy on yourself and remember you can always forgive and get back into peace if you find yourself uneasy, or upset. I hope these little thoughts help you in some way. If not, understand that you have helped me by listening and I'm very grateful to you.*

*From our beautiful "green country" which today is white, I send my love and good thoughts. Until next time, I remain your friend. —annie*

✧ ✧ ✧

My Dear Children, it is with pleasure that I come with a message of goodness. Let your hearts be filled with hope and faith, for never once are you separated from our Father who created this and all worlds. Let your whole being be filled with the hope that all things in your lives will be better. That what is transpiring in your life today is just. It is good and it is loving. I realize that not all blessings come cloaked in the appearance of goodness. Many times you seem to have problems, or difficulty. But for today, let us see that what appears to be a problem can truly be the greatest lesson and the greatest blessings that you have received.

Maintain faith and remember that faith is the substance which creates the good you seek. Faith is important because without faith you have nothing to build with. When we say faith is the substance, I mean that faith is the building blocks which the Spirit of God uses to create good in your life.

So how do you maintain faith? How do you increase your faith? You maintain your faith by using it. Faith, like the muscles in your body, will deteriorate if not used. Faith then is what is needed in today's world. The faith that will build and create the good that you seek. Faith that says, in spite of the appearances to the contrary, I trust that God will provide for my every need.

It takes only a small amount of true faith to build worlds and universes. So do not be dismayed with the appearance of difficulty or the appearance of wrong or bad. These are not true sight. It is the sight of fear. Fear tears and erodes faith. It is important to keep your faith as free of fear as you can. You do this by remembering that you now believe in God's eternal Love.

I have imparted over and over messages on God's Love and have shared with you how very much you are loved without judgment and without prejudices. This is Truth. My little children, God loves you and will keep you in His love. Have faith in this. Keep this thought in your mind when your fear for the future overcomes you. Nothing in your future is to be feared, not predicted tragedies, nor my own predictions for the future.

You live eternally, and so there is no need to fear anything in your future. You can always be maintained in His love and His protection. God loves; He loves you so much that it is not His desire that anyone would be outside of His love. But also God created you with free-will choice. He gives you His abilities. He has imbued you with His great capacity to build, to create, and to form. When you are learning to build out of faith, you are using God's creativity. You are using His clay, you are working in His studio and laboratory. Faith then is the belief that God is with you at all times. It is the belief that you are always surrounded by His love. It is the belief in God's Goodness and in His Wholeness.

Keep the faith, my little children. Allow only the thought that you are loved, protected, and guided to help you overcome the fears which assail your being like a storm. Let the thought that you are ever connected to His Wholeness free your mind to see possibilities instead of problems. Let the very Spirit of God infuse and imbue you with Whole Essences. Then you will put aside the fears for the future. You will turn away from the hopelessness that can overtake a person when he loses faith.

Until I return to you with a new message, please, my little children, keep the faith. Maintain hope in your heart and believe wholeheartedly in God's love. Faith in a loving Creator allows you to believe in yourself and in your abilities, because God is the Creator of all that is in your life when you turn to Him. Daily pray for faith and daily pray for your loved ones to maintain their faith.

God is whole, that means there is nothing lacking in Him. He is complete and total. All that you need you find in our Father. Hoping that things in your life will unfold in loving ways and become better is all that is needed to maintain faith. The future is bright when you can see that all things that come to you are lessons and are ways for God to have a better relationship with you.

Believe that no matter what the appearance, the outcome is and will be good. Believe that you are truly connected to a loving Father who only awaits your call. He is allowing you to choose and to decide. He is bringing you to wholeness one step at a time. Let this be the thoughts that fill your heart with joy and with deep pleasure. I am loving you each more than you know.

Mary, Mother of Jesus.

# 33

# Faith Creates Your Future

4/97

I RECENTLY RECEIVED A LETTER from friends in England requesting that I share my views and feelings about the period of grace that has been extended. My friends in England said two "great lightworkers" in England had become disillusioned when "The Plan" changed and have since chosen not to receive further information, cutting themselves off from others in their circle. This request is quite timely, since I'd just been a speaker at The Universal Lightworkers Conference in Houston. My talk was "The Responsibilities of a Lightworker." I pray with my friends about their concerns for their friends. God always works for our good, and when our future is delayed, it is good, and when it arrives as predicted . . . it is also good.

First about the delay in Mother Mary's predictions. I feel grateful and somewhat awed by the fact that we have delayed the predicted future. In Mary's Message to the World, Mother Mary said that the whole reason for giving these predictions was to affect the inner changes, which would effect the outer changes. I'm paraphrasing the passage in the book. We are doing good! We've been praying more; many more people have been working on their inner life, cleansing their hearts and minds from the things that keep us from peace. My prayer is that we (people all over the world) continue to do those things that will take us into the time of peace *with as few catastrophes as possible.* One of the most difficult things about sharing prophesy is that some people believe that, if the prophesy doesn't come true, you have failed. Mother Mary let me know right away that the predictions She gave were Hers, not mine. I was not responsible for them. I am simply the messenger and not the prophet, so perhaps it's been easier for me to detach from the predictions.

When the future is predicted and given as prophesy, it begins to change the future instantly. Awareness, we've been told, changes the future. When you first heard of the predictions, didn't you say instantly, "Oh, NO! This can't be," or something to that effect? That is an instant prayer and, because it stays in the consciousness, it becomes more focused. It is only natural not to want disasters in our future, and it is only natural to pray for a change in that kind of future.

In May of 1996, Mother Mary said, in the message for the June newsletter, that we are in a ten-year grace period, which can be increased to fifteen years. She also said that the year 2012 would be a monumental year. So we have done well; we've delayed the really bad disasters for at least that time period. Mother Mary said the weather would continue to be erratic and that we would still have natural disasters. To me, this means that the really bad stuff is delayed and minimized. So pat yourselves on the back; we are doing good, and let us renew our commitment to continue to pray, work on our inner self, and to love without judgment.

This takes me to the responsibilities of a lightworker. This term is used in some circles to denote people who are doing their spiritual work. I believe we are all lightworkers, whether we choose to do our spiritual work through one religion or another, or no religion at all. The only light we have to work with is our own. Our responsibility is the same as Mother Mary asked of all of us, whether we call ourselves by that term or not. We are to keep our inner light shining by clearing away the old debris of unresolved angers, envy, jealousy, resentments, and long-held fears and phobias.

We are reminded that Jesus said, "I am the light of the world, ye are the light of the world." He also said not to hide our light under a bushel. I feel that the "bushel" could easily be all the

## FAITH CREATES YOUR FUTURE

*unresolved angers and fears that keep us from being at peace, and loving ourselves and others without judgment. It's not lecturing, writing a book, or being known as a lightworker; it's doing the inner work of keeping our light bright, shining and lit at all times. We are like the person who runs a lighthouse. The lighthouse worker keeps things clean, supplies on hand, and is ready to shine the light when the night becomes foggy and the way seems unnavigable. Through their efforts ships and boats stay on course. The lighthouse worker doesn't set their course, or control their destination. He just keeps the light shining, knowing this is his job. We have the same responsibility to keep our inner light shining through prayer, resolving old angers, and facing our long-held fears. Most importantly, we remain responsible when we keep a forgiving and loving attitude. It's forgiveness that helps us live in peace, capable of loving unconditionally at all times. So today, let us give ourselves some well deserved credit. We know that as a people we are doing good when we can affect our future in the most minute way. We are doing good when we begin to live in peace. Remember what Mother Mary said to me about my son, David, "We will take care of the inside, and when the inside is right, the outside will take care of itself." Let's care for our inner life and pray that the outside will take care of itself in such a way that it's seen as miraculous.*

*Thanks for letting me share some thoughts; until next time I remain your friend. —annie*

My Dear Children, I come today to speak about faith and understanding. Many of you are feeling constrained by the future. You are concerned with what will be, how it will happen, and so many other concerns for food, shelter, or money. I bring the gift of renewed faith. Allow yourselves to be renewed daily through your prayers, and through your meditations. Let your minds be filled with joy because faith brings comfort, peace, and patience. Faith has many good by-products that are not only gifts but energizing to your spirit, mind, heart, and soul.

Faith is the substance that creates your future. To say you don't have faith, is to say you don't have life. Faith is a part of your being and needs to be nurtured and cherished. How many of you have faith that the laws of nature will continue to perform as they always have? You believe so deeply that when you close your eyes at night to rest, the sun and morning will follow the night, without any doubt. This is faith. You have faith in your ability to continue to think; you never doubt your capacity to love. Yet when you come to what you perceive as spiritual ideas, you doubt your faith. You doubt that you are connected to God. Many doubt they will have the money to continue to live life. One small set back, or large set back, financially and many of you are in despair. You think God has abandoned you. You forget to seek the lesson and gift these circumstances bring.

My dear children, you have faith. You have enough faith to keep planning for tomorrow and arising each morning to face what the day brings. You have the faith to go to sleep each night fully expecting the morning to come. You have faith, when you eat, your body is nourished without your instruction. You have faith that, when you plant seeds, they will reproduce of their own kind. You have faith that, when it rains, the sunshine will follow. You have faith enough to live, and faith enough to live fully.

Many of you are experiencing health problems. Have faith that as your body can find nourishment in the foods you eat, it will also have the ability to heal. If you have need of medical assistance, then by all means put your faith in the inner guidance and the medical person who is aiding you to become healthy. If you have relationship or family problems,

## FAITH CREATES YOUR FUTURE

have faith that the good will you have towards your loved ones will lead you to find ways of making peace. Have faith in your love and in your ability to love. Instead of railing against God, nature, the Universe, your religious teachings or leaders, your family . . . stand still and remember that you already have faith in yourself, in the life force that charges through you daily, and in the laws of nature. This is a beginning . . . to recognize the faith you already have. Never again say, "I lack faith." If you go to sleep each night expecting to arise in the morning, you have faith. It's enough faith to move mountains, to heal bodies, and to live peacefully. Remember what Jesus said if you have the faith of a mustard seed. You already have the faith of a mustard seed. The mustard seed is one tiny seed. When you recognize the faith that keeps you looking forward to a new day, you have faith . . . it is enough.

When you recognize that you already have faith, then you will find understanding. Understanding brings wisdom and new ideas. To be lost in despair because things are not going as you would have them go, or because there has been a decrease of love, good outcomes in relationships, family, business, finance, health, or spiritual awareness . . . is to close your eyes and not see the possibilities that are in front of you. Faith opens your mind to understand more fully. Understanding opens your eyes to see in a new light, with a new perspective and a new vision. How many times have you said, "I see! Why didn't I see this before?" This is understanding.

Once the scales of despair are removed from your eyes, your mind opens up to new possibilities. The very opening into the arena of full potential and total possibilities is you opening your mind to the work arena of God. Because the Father within is full of possibilities and total potential, your potential for new ideas is released, and with it circumstances, situations, people and places come into your life to fulfill and answer your prayers in miraculous ways. But first there has to be the recognition of faith. Your recognition comes when you are aware of the many ways you already have faith.

Understanding allows you to be ready to receive new ideas, new people, and new circumstances in your life. So many times people pray for good to come into their life and then close their eyes by denying their faith. They do not hold on to the little faith they have; instead they deny they have any faith at all. Now that you know that you do have faith, nurture it by affirming to yourself that you have the faith to move mountains. Let the results of your request go into that great arena of God's loving full potential and total possibility. Allow the results to come in God's own way and in His own time. Affirm that you have the faith to move mountains and the understanding to see the way as it is presented to you. Then be ready to act in faith. Be ready to see with full understanding what you need to do next. Be prepared to do the smallest thing even if you have done it before. Now when you perform the act, it will be done with full understanding and with renewed faith. Renew your faith daily through affirmations, understanding that God is not changed through your affirmations . . . you are. Pray daily to be ready to do what God directs you to do in order to live as you have chosen to live. Now, if you have not made choices, it is time you do. Understanding now that God is full potential and total possibilities, you see that God awaits your choices when you become spiritually aware. It is up to you to decide how to live your life. Do you seek truth, wisdom, love, healing, success, spiritual renewal, peace, or purpose? Then ask for it. But a major part of faith is surrender. It is your faith that allows you to be able to surrender your request and petition to God. It is your understanding that keeps you strong in the belief that God is good and only gives good to His creation. Remember, it will happen in God's time, which is different from earth time. Your prayers will be answered, and you will see the answers clearly. You will not miss the miracle, the wonder, and the majesty of working with God. You will spring to life with renewed vigor and a deeper love for all of God's creation.

Thank you for listening to my words. I am loving you as you continue to grow in faith and understanding.

Mary, Mother of Jesus.

# 34

## *You Can Make a Difference*

6/97

A COUPLE OF THINGS HAVE HAPPENED RECENTLY which are serving as a way for me to remember that judgment is not the way to love unconditionally. For example, often people have preconceived ideas of who I am, how I should be, how I should act, and what motivates me. And more often than I care for, a few people place me on a pedestal. You know what happens when you are up on a high, small place . . . you can fall off! I quickly fall and crash, but it's usually at the expense of a developing friendship. But it isn't funny when people who I've considered friends make a judgment based on a preconceived idea that I should now act like a saint. It doesn't upset me any more, but it has given me the opportunity to speak my truth.

Just because I receive messages from Mother Mary doesn't imbue me with any special spiritual powers or attributes. I haven't turned into a saint, nor do I keep "the pained Christ" look on my face. I make mistakes, I disappoint people, I get angry, I'm human with all of humanity's emotions and frailties. The receiving of the messages is very special and this in no way belittles that. I am truly blessed by these communications. But I've not magically turned into a great spiritual person because of it. I've had to do my healing, in my own way. I'm not Mary, nor am I in any way the Blessed Mother's representative. Another thing that happens more often than I like is that people often call me Mary. My name is Annie. I do not *represent Her, nor am I infused with Mary's spirit. Nor are Mary and I the same, as a few misguided people have stated.*

*I'm very aware of my shortcomings and I know that I'm still working to love everyone, unconditionally, all the time, even those I don't particularly like. Please do not confuse the message with me. Often I say I'm just the Fed Ex or UPS person for Mother Mary. That may sound sacrilegious to some people, but it's the best way I can describe my role. I don't exemplify the message, nor am I the message. I'm trying just like you to put the message into effect so it can make a difference in my life. Mother Mary asked me to encourage you to work on your connection to God in your own way. So when I say I'm learning something, it doesn't mean I've "got it," but that I'm working on it. Together we can encourage each other. Together we can make a difference in our own lives, and in our loved one's lives. Then, together we will make a difference in the consciousness of mankind.*

*When we fall into the old habit of judging, either ourselves or others, we are not loving unconditionally. Usually when we judge, we don't see the good in people, or ourselves. We focus on the mistakes, flaws, failures, and the times either we or others act in unloving ways. Mother Mary says God loves unconditionally and to be at peace we are to love ourselves and each other the same way. For me this means I monitor how I view other people. Judging was an integral part of my family of origin's dynamics, and it's been difficult to set the habit aside. There are times Byron will say, "That's judging," when I think I'm making an observation. It's one thing to observe and another to place blame. Placing blame is what I do when I'm judging. How many times do we say, "How could he/she do that?" meaning that the person is "wrong, bad, or lacking." Have you heard a statement like this, "Look at him/her . . . that's not how a spiritual person should act?" This is judgment, and it's also spiritual arrogance.*

*Once we asked Mother Mary how we could tell who is spiritual and who is not. She told us there was no way while we are on earth to tell who is truly spiritual and who isn't. She said the most spiritual person in our city (which was Dallas) could live in the worst part of town and be considered the worst drunk in town. One other time when I was having a problem forgiving, She said, "The greatest gift one soul can give another is to come into their life to be their nemesis." This gives a whole new perspective on the difficult people in our lives.*

*We are in this life experience together, and we all experience imperfection. At any given time mistakes are being made. Our goal is to love unconditionally, like our Divine Parent/God loves us. He loves us without limit, without judgment, withholding no part of Himself. We are loved more than we can understand, and more than we can imagine. It's our happiness and good that we withhold by judging harshly. My commitment to myself and to my Creator is that I will do all I can to learn to love as He does. I love by saying, "I love you," withholding no part of myself. The human part of me may be stung by criticism or judgment, but this too shall pass away. What never dies is the love we share.*

*Thank you for allowing me to state my truth and for your continued support. I appreciate each of you, so with love I remain your friend. —annie*

◇ ◇ ◇

My Dear Children, it is with pleasure that I come to you in love. I hear your anguished pleas for help. Many are in confusion as to why God causes or allows bad things to happen. God loves. In His great love, He has given you freedom of choice. If you do not make your own choices, other people's choices will determine circumstances and situations to happen that could affect you. God loves, without judgment, without reservation. His loves flows freely to all people, those who appear to be living spiritual lives and those who are not. God loves you no matter your circumstances or the conditions of your life.

God's love is more than you can understand, more than you can comprehend, more than you can envision. God's love is pure energy; it is pure love that has nothing but good imbued into every atom. God's love is Himself, coming to you in the most pleasant, comfortable, and energizing ways. So when you see hunger, disease, cruelty, abuse, or violence, understand these conditions are not created by God . . . but by humanity. Humanity will heal them through the efforts of individual people, working one by one to recreate heaven on earth through love.

Cry out, my children, if you so desire. Become enraged; recognize the injustice of these and many other undesirable conditions. Yet understand God is not the cause; humanity is the cause of these conditions. Humanity can correct them. These conditions will be corrected in love. To judge another person harshly is to perpetuate these conditions. When you speak badly about another person, injustice continues to be fed. To become immune to the suffering of other people and see them as less than you, is to feed the injustices of this world. When you deny your own emotions and try to hide your meanness or harshness, you water these conditions. When you abuse yourself or others, you cultivate violence in the world. As you place conditions on your love, you stamp out kindness and poison the wells of human kindness.

You have the ability and the power through prayer to correct these conditions so they will be eliminated for all time. You have the means in your hand to bring an end to world hunger, not only by giving food, or money to buy food, but through prayer and through daily loving actions. You can end disease not only through new and better treatments or medicines, but end it for all time through your love as you daily pray and treat each other with gentleness. You can bring cruelty to an end through your prayers and by loving all people, no matter how they act or react, what they believe or do not believe. You can cease the wars in families and in nations through your prayers and through your acceptance of each other, loved ones and strangers alike. You can stop the injustices of the world through your prayers, and by ceasing to judge yourself or another harshly.

All this is possible, because you have the ability to live in peace. It will happen as each individual begins and continues to live in inner peace, prayer, and a heart filled with unconditional love. It is your joy to be a peacemaker; it is your pleasure to live a love-filled life. It will be an honor to give the future generations a world free of cruelty, violence, disease, and hunger. You can make a difference, my children. You have in your hands the means, abilities, method, and knowledge to make a huge difference in the world. You alone can fulfill humanity's destiny of peace. You are needed; don't think for one minute that you can't make a difference. Your prayers are powerful when they are backed by a love-filled life. Remember that it is a life guided, supplied and imbued with unconditional love that makes the difference.

My little children, I am only asking of you that which you are fully capable of giving. You can live in peace. You can love without judgment and without bias. It will require of you dedication, commitment, and effort. It will take being dedicated to prayer. Pray daily, and I ask that each of you pray one hour a day as a minimum. Meditate and listen to the silent voice of God daily. Give yourself time to be silent. Only in true silence of the soul will you fully communicate with the Father, who is within you. Listen with your inner ear and hear the murmuring of your soul as it glories in its Divine communication with its Source of Life, Love, and all Good.

Remember always that prayer is talking to God. Talk to Him as you would a beloved parent, or a trusted friend. Talk to Him in honesty, for God alone can look into your heart of hearts. He sees your motivation, commitment, intention, and honesty. He hears your longings, inner yearnings, and your emotions as they display your reactions to life's situations. God feels your suffering, concerns, angers, fears, and your hopes and dreams. Nothing is withheld from God's view. Why would you persist in thinking that you cannot be truthful with Him? It is useless to be dishonest with God. Step out of the illusion of denial and take a good look at your life, at your motivations and at how you live now. Speak to God in your own way, whether that way is the prayers learned through your religion or just plain talking as you do to yourself. Please don't become impassive because you can't decide the right way to pray. God just wants to hear from you, in your own words or through learned prayers and ritual. He is like a loving parent who is waiting patiently to hear from His children.

God loves you and treats each of you as if you were His most precious creation. This is how God treats everyone. Understand that we all are God's most precious creation, we are all one in Him. We live because God lives. He loves completely and totally, and He loves you now. Allow His love to fill your heart, your life and your day with joy. Begin each day with the gentle reminder that God loves you. It doesn't matter to Him what is happening in your life, what your circumstances are, or what the situation of your life is ... God loves you. He sees your full potential, the total creation which is you. He knows you inside out, and is just as proud of you when you think you are winning, or being very spiritual, or very religious, as He does when you feel lost and without hope.

Love each other, pray one for the other. Be of good cheer and seek the truth of your life. Let your heart be healed of all malice, resentments, and fears. Your prayers added to others' prayers can cause miracles to happen. The world can enter a thousand years of peace in joy, instead of heartbreak.

I am loving you, my children. I am loving you and praying with you for your good health, and inner peace. I am with you in prayer and in love.

Mary, Mother of Jesus.

# The Real Gift

8/97

As I was preparing for our open house, *I began to worry about how this would all work out. I was thinking of the logistics of accommodating people in our home. I was feeling very responsible for the people who would come and how they would feel about the experience. Then Mother Mary whispered in my ear, "They are not coming for you, Annie." This statement made me feel better; it took all the responsibility and worry off me. I again realize that it's not my work. It's God's and Mary's Work. I simply have a small part in it. I have been hearing the words, "I'm gathering my children." What that means, I don't know.*

*Once again I'm reminded, it's not about me, it's about being willing to follow the prompting of Spirit. It's also about surrendering all my concerns and worry, and allowing God to work through me. I'm not in charge of the gathering. It's in Mother Mary's hands. She is the one directing the outcome. Whatever happens, or doesn't happen, will be good. As we gather to pray and meditate as a group, we will be participating in a most powerful experience, because we come together in love. We love Mother Mary, we love God, and we are loving ourselves, and our fellow man. To gather in love is powerful; it's also very healing.*

*Many times Mother Mary has said to me that the only way to bring peace into the world is that I live in peace and encourage others to live in peace. She said, "Peace will come to earth through the hearts of man." She was speaking about inner peace, and it's mankind to whom She refers, which includes everyone, regardless of gender. It's not always easy to have inner peace. For me it means that when I'm out-of-sorts, I get myself back into a peaceful state of mind, willingly and quickly. It also means that when I become agitated, I can no longer afford to spend time upset. I realize it's imperative to quickly do all I can to get back into inner peace. Some of us have family members who, for one reason or another, are difficult to deal with and keep our inner peace intact. Sometimes we have to distance ourselves from them for our own peace of mind. It's a difficult decision to make and to carry through. Even if we cannot tolerate any contact with them, or can only tolerate short periods of time, we can continue to love them, pray for them, and hope that their highest good comes to them.*

*Many times I look at the situation that has upset me and I find, much to my distress, that it is me that needs to change or adjust. And then there are times I find all the situation requires is for me to state my needs. One of my shortcomings is that I have a problem voicing my needs. Instead, I give a voice to my displeasure and do things like be short-tempered, or speak in short, terse sentences, letting everyone know I'm upset. Often I cannot say what is bothering me, sometimes I don't know, and sometimes I don't want to face what is bothering me. When I'm out-of-sorts and don't know why, I start looking—seeking earnestly because I don't feel good in this frame of mind. Staying upset doesn't lead to peace; in fact it can lead to more turmoil and sometimes to resentments and other negative emotions.*

*So living in peace, as I see it, is setting my direction and headings towards peace, and making sure that my underlying intention is to love unconditionally. When I'm not living in peace, I know I need to take some action, change, or adjust in order to once again be going in the direction of peace. I know instantly when I'm out of peace because it feels terrible to be out of a peaceful state of mind. After you have lived in peace a while, you will gladly do whatever it takes to be back in peace.*

## THE REAL GIFT

*One other thing about peace, it requires that I surrender to God, either the situation, the people in the situation, or something about the situation in order to be back in peace. I find it difficult each time to surrender. It takes me going through the process of surrender. Each time I surrender, I tell myself it's getting easier to surrender. I don't know if it is, but I like to think it is. I'm assured that I'm doing my best, and that's all that Mother Mary says we can do. Just do your very best to live in peace, and to let love be the basis of your life. This doesn't mean you will always feel peaceful and loving, but it means you will recognize quickly when you are not feeling peaceful or loving. Then you will head back into that direction again. So if you lose your temper, become short-tempered, or upset, don't criticize or judge yourself harshly. Just let it go and set your sights in the direction of peace and love again. Let the judgment stop at the first sign of criticism.*

*This is the analogy that I use to explain how I go about living in peace. You are driving a car and you let go of the steering wheel; the car goes all over the road and may go off the road. That's not the time to get angry and upset with yourself. You don't want to keep your hand off the steering wheel criticizing yourself. It's time to quickly take hold of the steering wheel and steer the car back into its lane and correct direction. This is how I see living in peace and being out of peace. When I am out of peace, I need to quickly shut up and get myself going in the right direction. Just like the car when I lose my direction, all I need is to steer myself towards peace, without taking the time to criticize, or browbeat myself.*

*Thank you once again for letting me share some thoughts.*

*—annie*

◇ ◇ ◇

M<small>Y</small> D<small>EAR</small> C<small>HILDREN</small>, I come today with my heart full of love. I am pleased with those of you who have been changing your lives for the better. I am proud of those of you who have been working to clear from your heart and mind all unresolved anger and lingering fear. This is helping the world to change for the better. We are all interconnected through God's love. What one person does affects the whole world. How do you help others? The first step to helping others is to help yourself. You help yourself by changing from an angry, fearful person, to one who lives with the intention of loving without judgment or reservation. Then you are ready to help others.

The best way to help others is to support them with your prayers. Pray for your loved ones to have good in their lives. Because when you ask for good, you are asking for more of God's essence to manifest in their lives. Pray for friends and your enemies, or the people who are against you in any way. Prayer is the best gift you can give another. When you pray, do not decide what that person needs. It isn't up to you to make these kinds of decisions. Pray simply that good come to them and that they have good experiences and good in every area of their lives. Then let God and the person work out how that good will manifest in their lives.

After you have prayed, you are ready to do good deeds. You are ready to help others who are ready to be helped. Be sure that when you help, you are in reality helping the person and not simply allowing them to continue to ignore their problems. There are times when it is appropriate to give a person food and there are times when it would do the person more good to learn to grow, or earn his food. Be prudent in your giving. Be sure that you give for the benefit of the person you wish to help and not to make yourself feel good. Think about what your intent is in giving. Is it to do good deeds? Is it to help a fellow human in his time of need? Or is it to ensure that you have a place in heaven?

# THE REAL GIFT

Intent, motivation, and purpose are important ingredients in giving. Equally important as why you give, is how you give. Is your heart filled with non-judgmental love? Is your underlying foundation in your life love? Do you come to the act of giving in love? Do you see the person who is to receive your help as needy or lacking in some way? If you think that person doesn't understand, either how to make a good living, or how to rely on God, you find him lacking. If you think the person you are helping is beneath you intellectually, monetarily, educationally or in any other way, your giving is lacking. The giving is lacking the unseen gift that comes from a loving, cheerful heart.

When you give with a heart filled with non-judgmental love, you give from the heart, soul, spirit, and therefore it is infused with the energy of love. Be sure that when you decide to help another person, it is the kind of help that person needs, wants, can accept, and that the gift is given in love, and with joy. There is more to giving that handing out a loaf of bread, or an amount of money. The real gift comes with prayer, love, and joy.

It is so important that you love yourself without judgment, without reservations, and without limits. It is important that you learn to respect yourself, your beliefs, your choices and your decisions. It is important that you honor and love your family, even if they are unloving towards you. It is important for you to awake each morning ready to love, filled with joy, and ready to forgive any slight. In this way you are living as a true child of God.

My dear children, this is something that is easily within your capability to live. Your very essence is love. It is when the person forgets to love, or hasn't been taught the many aspects of love, that he becomes fearful or angry. Accept yourself as you are today and then accept the people whom you help as they are today. When you can love yourself without judgment, then you are prepared to love others as God does.

Too many times people think I can't help anyone; I don't have either money, time, energy, the means, or the way. But everyone has the time to say a prayer. Always remember this is the best gift to offer. Everyone has the energy to love if they have love in their hearts at all times. Everyone can acknowledge another human being with a smile, a nod of the head, or a common courtesy. It doesn't take a lot to help. It takes a willingness to love people. People want to be acknowledged and accepted as living, breathing, human beings.

When you can accept people, really accept them without trying to change them, then you are loving as God loves. God gives everyone the freedom to choose, and to make their own decisions. He accepts that you are in the situation of your choice. He awaits you to ask for His help. This is how to accept your loved ones, friends, and all people. Remember, they have the right to choose how to live their life, how to believe, whom to love, and when to call on God.

What do you do when you see a loved one in the throes of an addiction, or in a behavior pattern that depletes their soul of love, joy, and health? You pray, you pray, and you pray more. You tell them your concerns with love and offer to help in anyway that they feel is appropriate for them. You do this once, then you make no comment with your voice or your face. You cannot change another person. If you preach to them, thinking this is how to get them to change, you are acting in vain. You can pray and love them unconditionally. You can be ready to help when called upon. But with people who have addictions, be sure your help isn't the kind of help that aids them to stay in their addiction. Be sure that, if there are emotional or mental health problems, you have help from a trained person, or doctor in that field.

If you find that you are loving a person who has a void within their heart, remember you cannot fill that void. Only they can heal the issues that have caused the void. As those issues are being healed, the void will become less pronounced. Again pray for them, asking for good to enter their lives. Pray for your loved one to see and know the truth that will set them free.

There are many ways to love, these are but a few. I urge you to live with an underlying basis of love, a heart filled with joy, and an inner peace. This is how to help the world, as you help yourself, and your loved ones. You are my beloved children, I am well pleased with each of you, as you learn to love without judgment, without reservation, and without limit. Thank you for listening to me.

Mary, Mother of Jesus.

# 36

## Live in Peace

10/97

To say our Mary Prayer Day and open house was a success *is an understatement. It went beyond success to pure enjoyment. It was such a pleasure and joy to have shared with so many loving people. On Friday, August 15, 1997, we congregated at Lake Tenkiller, near our home. People came from across the country; it was an amazing and beautiful gathering. Before sunset, we got quiet and prayerful in attitude. The sun spun and danced. There were bursts of color. Many felt the presence of Mary, Blessed Mother. Some of us had the blessing of seeing Her, in my case as the standing Madonna. It was an awesome and awe-inspiring experience. One lady wrote a poem, that is available on our Internet web page,\* along with pictures Byron took at the lake.*

*On Saturday and Sunday people came to our home. They shared their stories and insights, talked, and then we all prayed. Everyone treated each other with kindness, love and respect.*

*Saturday night we had a bonfire, per Mother Mary's request. Some sat or stood close to the fire and meditated. The rest of us sat further away. People talked to each other quietly. We used the fire to burn away the habits, thoughts, attitudes, and beliefs we no longer wanted to keep. Mostly people talked quietly among themselves.*

*Sunday we held our regular meditation session and read from* Messages to Our Family. *We prayed and meditated. It was a very loving and uniting session. Many in the group said it felt like we are family. People exchanged stories, experiences, and addresses. The whole weekend felt like an ideal family reunion. And in reflecting, we are family. We are the human family. That weekend our branch of the human family had a wonderful time with Mother Mary and each other.*

*At this time, my challenge is to accept my body, just as it is. Years ago I made a decision to take a medication that I knew was dangerous and had long lasting effects. When I honestly recall the situation (raising three teenagers alone), I know that if I had to do it again, under the same conditions, I would make the same decision. It helps me accept the consequences of the choice I made. It was the best choice and decision I could make in my particular situation. I know that with God all things are possible. I pray that I can be relieved of the results of this decision and enjoy a healthy and energetic body. But whatever the answer, I pray to accept what is happening now.*

*Mother Mary said that acceptance is love, and it is peace, too. So many times, in order to live in peace, we need to accept the consequences of past choices. I am loving myself when I accept past decisions and the result of those decisions. It would be anti-loving to berate my choice or decision. Acceptance brings me into a peaceful state of mind, which is my goal.*

*Life is one experience after another. I've had wonderful experiences over my sixty years on earth. I'm grateful for each of them, both good ones and bad ones. The terms good and bad have changed for me. I don't always think in terms of good and bad. I've had enough experiences to know that there is always good in every situation, even those that are painful or embarrassing.*

*I love my life, I love the giver of All Life more. I look forward to more experiences like the ones I had on that amazing and loving weekend—we opened our home, and welcomed the rest of our family in. Look forward to every experience—they each bring good, if we remember to look for the good in them. Until next time, I remain your friend. —annie*

M‍y Dear Children, I come in love and peace. Peace is your future, not just a possibility. Love and peace are your clear essence. The love you seek, the comfort, acceptance, and appreciation that you so desire, are all within your heart of hearts. It is in the deep inner recess of your soul, that you find your true essence. Your essence is the image and likeness of God. What is true of God is true of your image and your likeness.

It is your true nature to live in peace. This is God's truth. You were created to live in peace, be loving beings, be happy, joyful, and healthy. So you wonder how come so many are born with infirmities. It is between that person and God why they have chosen to come into the world to suffer the indignities of an imperfect body. God created their spirit, their soul, which is not suffering or imperfect. They were created to live in peace. What keeps many from inner peace is that they seek flaws and find them.

Every person can be loving, but first they will need to learn to love themselves, unconditionally. What keeps many from experiencing love is that they have not learned to love themselves. Therefore they reside outside the circle of inner love and cannot experience what is lacking in their heart. Every person can be happy, and joyful. What harms people the most is to remain unforgiving of themselves and others. Your soul is healthy, but many choose to use health issues to resolve old hurts, to rectify old angers. This is their choice. It is not a wrong choice; it is simply their choice. The truth, God's truth, is that in you nothing is lacking because in God, nothing is lacking. You can be loving, healthy, happy individuals who live in peace.

How do you begin to live in peace? Do all you can to stop any inner war taking place within your body, mind, heart, or being. Then do all you can to end family wars. Let your countenance reflect your inner peace and love as you relate to others. Your facial expression can lead a situation to peace or to discord. Many times in a disruptive situation when one person comes in peace, with peace reflected in their being, they begin to turn the discordant situations towards peace. You are the peacemakers. You are called forth today to live your life with a deep, abiding inner peace. This is how to lead people to peace, not by talking about it, but by living it.

When you live in inner peace, you think peaceful thoughts, your feelings are peaceful, and your behavior is peaceful. Peaceful people do not judge or acknowledge anything bad in other people. You look at them in love and see their true nature, which is goodness, love, joy, and peace. When you are peaceful, you speak truth compassionately and you hear the truth as it is spoken. Love opens your senses and allows you to see clearly and lovingly, hear with an open mind and heart, feel with your whole being, smell aromas that are not of this earth, and taste the living waters of God. Love and peace combined are healing and soothing in every situation and circumstance.

Do everything you can to live in peace. Rejoice when you can accept yourself and others without conditions or judgments. Marvel at the many opportunities that come to you, to live in peace. Let your actions, and behaviors reflect the inner peace as it grows within your being. Do this so that you can live up to your goal of ushering in the new era of peace.

Be prepared for every eventuality in your future by learning to live from a heart filled with love and a deep, inner peace. This way of living enables you to know the truth. When people become fearful and panic due to rumors, you will know the truth and know when to act, what to do, and how to care for yourself and others, as this is your calling. Let not your heart be filled with any lingering fears, and then you will not react to the fears which reside in other people's hearts. Look within your heart of hearts for the truth in every situation.

To be prepared for any eventuality, first learn to love yourself and others without judgment or reservation. Second, prepare physically as you are guided to do. Collect supplies, water, food, fuel, blankets, and the things which will help you, your loved ones, and others. Learn ways to care for yourself and others, become knowledgeable in your preparation. Remain in a state of preparedness; do not waver or falter in this. Use your common sense, that instinct for survival that is within mankind. Be prudent in your preparations and do this with a peaceful heart and a loving intention. Daily do all that you can to live your life in love and inner peace, trusting God to guide you in all things. Then you will be able to face whatever comes your way. It will not matter if the future brings earthquake, storm, flood, disease, man-made accidents, war, or even the moving of continents. Nothing will disturb your inner peace, your loving heart, or your trust in God. Prepare because it is wise to do so.

Daily act and react from a heart filled with peaceful love, and not from a fearful nature. Do away with any lingering fears; resolve anger. Clear your heart and mind of all that keeps you from loving yourself, from inner peace, and from trusting in the goodness of God.

Trust that God's love will guide you in all things. Then daily learn to listen to your heart and mind. Keep your communion with God daily. Trust that when you are in close connection to the Father within, you will hear, understand,

and be able to follow His guidance. Trust your knowing, for out of a knowing heart comes peace, out of a knowing mind comes direction, and out of the knowingness of your soul, you know your true nature.

My little children, when you are prepared as I have requested, it will not be necessary for you to anticipate future events. When you try to anticipate the future, you concentrate on outer events, and could begin to forget the most important preparation. The most important preparation is to remain close to God through prayer and meditation—to see His goodness in the world instead of a dire future. You could focus your attention so much on the future, that you forget to see the blessings of this day, the joy of living and the love you have now. Be prepared, yes, but not to the exclusion of your inner connection to God.

Let nothing keep you from God—not fear, anger, guilt, shame, or anything. In reality nothing keeps you from God because He lives within your being as He does in every person. God lives in this world; it is His life force that animates. So in God's truth you are never apart from God, but in your thinking and daily living, you form the illusion of being apart from God. The depleting emotions and depleting issues of your life give you this illusion of separation. So resolve the depleting issues, find the inner joy of living a loving, joyful, and peaceful life. This is my request. This is my prayer and desire for each of you. Thank you for listening to my request. I am loving each of you today.

Mary, Mother of Jesus.

# 37

## *Peace Is Serenity*

12/97

CAN YOU BELIEVE ANOTHER YEAR IS WINDING DOWN? *It seems just like yesterday that we were enjoying peach blossoms in our orchard. Today most of the leaves are gone and there are only a few colorful trees displaying their beauty. It's time to take notice, be thankful, and prepare for the Holidays.*

*It's usually at this time that we like to write letters of appreciation to each other. There is no one, outside of my immediate family that I appreciate more than you—our newsletter friends and supporters. You have written and called to share special tidbits, stories, poems, and experiences. I've taken them to heart and read every letter. Your letters, calls, and prayers have helped me tremendously. You've truly been friends, neighbors, and supporters. Your prayers, interest and love have blessed me more than you know. I'm grateful to God for you. My love and blessings are sent with this newsletter, along with my wishes for you and your family to have a wonderful Holiday Season. Merry Christmas, Happy New Year, and Happy Hanukkah.*

*Since about September, I've been feeling very disconnected. Intellectually I know, I'm never separated from God. He is my breath, heartbeat, and life, so I can't be disconnected. But in my emotions and body, I feel the disconnection. At times it feels like I am floating in a huge void. A Colorado friend calls this "the dark night of the soul."* I think that is a good description of what I sometimes feel. According to cliches, it's always darkest before the dawn. This cliche doesn't make me feel any better, but it has given me food for thought.

A few years ago when I was feeling this way and was quite concerned, I spoke to a friend about it and she reminded me that God created out of the Void . . . with His word. So maybe this is what is happening. It's time to re-create my life and myself, with my words. This condition may feel bad, until I take the judgment away and look at the truth of a void. When viewed as a process for creation, or for creating, then it can't be bad. Once again, I'm reminded to leave the judgment off and seek the blessing in every situation and experience.

When I sat down a few days ago to begin this letter, I couldn't think of a thing to write about. Today a newsletter subscriber/friend called and was experiencing the same void. She answered my prayer of what to write about. I'm told to be honest with you, even if it's something that I would prefer to keep quiet. Mother Mary said it's through the sharing of my experiences that I encourage you to keep seeking the truth. This is my intention. It certainly isn't to complain, as was suggested a couple of times by callers.

I think it's a time for reevaluation, and for re-creating. It's really important to keep reminding myself that I am never apart from God and His love. No matter what I am feeling, I am still breathing and living. I'm as connected when I feel the connection and experience phenomena, as when I don't feel it. My spirit rejoices that the outer feelings are not God's Truth, but mankind's truth. My soul exhales peace when I remember that God is with me, no matter what condition, situation, or experience I'm facing. I remember that I'm more than this body, and that's a lot when the body is rebelling, big time. I also recall that I'm more than my feelings, more than my thoughts, and more than my history, and more than my experiences. My life is a gift and I dedicate it to The Source of All That Is. And at times my spirit is free to run through the Universe and at times my spirit is tied to earth.

I'm trying very hard to focus on making a new plan, creating a new me. As my therapist keeps reminding me when I need to go *through a painful memory, "Stay in the struggle." When I stay in the struggle, the condition or situation seems to evaporate, like a morning mist. It's my job to keep working this out for myself. And that's the truth! Each of us have to work things out for ourselves. No one else can do it for us. Sometimes we would like to find a guru or spiritual person who will take on our inner work. Or we pray for it to be wiped away as if by magic, but it doesn't work that way. Even the Buddha had to sit in deep contemplation and meditation for years in order to get "IT." He found what he was seeking inside of himself.*

*Over the past few months I've found myself singing songs that have "rejoice" as the theme. I guess I could say that being in the void is a time to rejoice, even if it feels terrible and lonely. I "can" make new choices and reevaluate and re-create my life according to my desires and wishes. All of us can, isn't that enough to rejoice over? We can begin again anytime we want, not only when we are in the void, but when we want to make a change. What a gift and blessing!*

*Once again, thank you for giving me this opportunity to work this out with you. This letter has given me the opportunity to put into words what has been in my heart for days and it helps it all become concrete in my mind. We love you and are aware how fortunate we are to have you in our life. Until next time I remain,*
*—annie*

⬥ ⬥ ⬥

M<small>Y</small> D<small>EAR</small> C<small>HILDREN</small>, I come to you in peace, with the request that you stay in peace. I ask that you believe in peace and live in peace. Let the song flow through you that rang out so long ago when I was blessed by becoming mother to Jesus. That night the angels sang, "Peace on earth, Goodwill to men." Let this be your song, your goal, and your prayer.

Believe in peace with your whole being. Believe in peace to the extent that you live your inner life in peace. Let your inner self become peaceful within your heart. Where there is any deterrent to peace—settle it, resolve it, forgive it. Let all your thoughts, all your motivations, be based on peace; with love filling your heart of hearts, you will be instrumental in realizing peace on earth. All the peace of God, that ever was, is here. For many, it is not in your lives, nor your hearts, and fails to be in your lives. It is important that you believe that peace is here. When you believe that peace is attainable, then you will find ways to live in peace. In your hearts, there is much to forgive and much to resolve. Whatever the deterrent to peace, understand that you have the capability to resolve, settle, and forgive. It is within your realm of possibilities to live in peace. You were created for peaceful living.

Make it your goal to live in inner peace and to extend that peace to your outer arena. Let your everyday events be peaceful. When there is conflict, settle the conflict with the awareness that peace is your goal. Peace is more important that your pride. Living in inner peace is how to leave a better world to your children and your loved ones. Seek to clear away the debris of fear, angers, and violence in your life. You teach more by example than with your words. This is true of your children and it is certainly true of your neighbors. Where there has been family wars, bring a peaceful solution. Where there has been inner conflict, turn to a peaceful settlement. Where there has been the ravages of inner turmoil, stay in prayer for forgiveness to bring peace. This is my request, it is my prayer that each of you learn to live in peace, to lead lives that are truly peaceful within and without.

During this time of celebration of Jesus' birth, I ask that you remember to love, as he did. I ask that you remember not to judge. I ask that you become still and listen to the voice of God. He tells you of ways to bring peace into your lives. For some of you it may mean healing an addiction or an old trauma. It may mean resolving old angers and making peace with your past. For others it may be in accepting life as it has been given to you. For most people it is in forgiving that you find peace.

Forgive yourselves foremost. Forgive the past; let the past stay buried. Too often you forgive the past and then resurrect it. Each time this happens you will need to begin the process of forgiving until it is no longer recalled in any manner. Forgive the world's people for all the wars taking place in this world. But the saddest wars in this world are family wars. So often family members fight each other. Many sit in churches trying to worship. I tell you as long as you hold one thing against a loved one, you cannot worship God in spirit and in truth. Take the opportunity this season gives you to resolve old family issues.

Forgive others; it is not your place to judge. Forgiveness will be not be needed when people cease judging each other. Forgiveness is the tool to bring peace to this world. Set aside your judgments. Do not acknowledge the differences in religions, people, or cultures. Instead acknowledge only the similarities between you and all people. Concentrate on the similarities, allowing open dialogue for accord.

My dear children, peace is more than setting aside differences, it is more than stopping wars, it is more than a cessation of vile speech. Peace comes from within, and until you have a peaceful heart, you cannot have peace. Too often people associate peace with no war, but peace is no inner war, no inner conflict, no inner deterrent to you loving yourself and others unconditionally. Peace is serenity. It is being serene in your mind, your heart, and in your body. It is reacting from this serenity and not from pain, anger, or fear.

## PEACE IS SERENITY

When your heart is filled with serenity, you will only react in peace. Serenity then is your goal to inner peace.

Once again I ask that you use the "Prayer of Serenity" as your guide. Accept the things you cannot change. One of the things you cannot change is each other. There is more inner conflict than warranted because people try to change each other. You want to dictate how your loved ones should live their lives. When in God's truth, each person is free to be themselves. Accept the things about yourself that cannot be changed. Stop the inner conflict over age, stature, culture, race, and all the other things you cannot change. When you see that the things you cannot change are not really that important, then you will have an easier time accepting them as truth. You are who you are, and no amount of wishing allows you to be someone else. Love yourself, honor who you are, accept yourself in your entirety. Be kind, compassionate, and determined to be serene. Then you forgive, accept, resolve, settle, and adjust to any condition or situation in your life that cannot be changed.

Have the courage to change the things you can. These things are certainly the issues of the heart, the obsessions of the mind, the addictions of the soul. Many of you have difficult issues to settle, much pain to heal, and terrible rages to resolve. Understand, my dear ones, that you can do this with God's help. He awaits your request for help in each situation. Listen to your inner guidance. He will guide you in the best way for you to become peaceful. Set aside your pride, look within, do your best. This is what you can do to become peaceful.

But most of all, know there is a difference in what can be changed and what cannot be changed. Pray for the wisdom to always know the difference. Seek to find the truth of your situation. Pray for others to find the truth of their situations. They will find ways to heal any condition. Wisdom is yours. Deep within you is the wisdom you seek. God placed deep within your heart of hearts all of His goodness. His love, wisdom, knowledge, understanding, peace, strength, courage, and His power are within you. Remember that Jesus said, "The kingdom of Heaven is within you." This is where to find your answers.

Pray for your world. Pray for the people involved in any warring situation. Pray for both sides in every altercation. Peace is not a national goal; it is worldwide goal. Pray for your enemies, as well as your friends. Pray for those who will not or cannot forgive you. It is more important to forgive than you to judge. I am praying that you live in peace and fulfill the song, "Peace on earth, Goodwill to men."

Mary, Mother of Jesus.

# 38

## Be Faithful in Your Prayers

2/98

WE ARE INTO A NEW YEAR *and hopefully you have found that everything is changing for the better.*

*It's incredible to me that I'm not only going to see the century change, but a millennium too. I remember my grandmother talking about something that had happened in the last century and I'd feel like I did when someone talked about B.C. times. It felt like that was so long ago. I can envision my grandchildren saying to their grandchildren, "In the last millennium, blah, blah, blah." I'm getting very excited about it.*

*We can affect how this new millennium enters. Mother Mary gave some grave predictions in Her original message, which have been delayed and minimized. I have no doubt that as we work within our lives to change our inner belief from a belief steeped in fear to a belief based on love, we can minimize and delay things further. She said that some things can't be changed. Instead of worrying about what can be, and what can't be changed, I'm concentrating on prayer and inner peace. I encourage you to concentrate on all the good things in life, like: love, peace, joy, and wisdom.*

*Mother Mary instructed all of us, in Her original message, to be ready for any future event. Byron and I have prepared physically and continue to prepare spiritually. The physical preparation is something that can be accomplished with time and money, then, for the most part, it's done. You can forget it and be at peace. But the spiritual preparedness is something that takes daily work. It takes prayer and scrupulous honesty. I have the bad habit of denying the things I would rather not face or see. Knowing this is part of my make-up, I need to be scrupulous. You may not need to be so exacting. Do what needs to be done in order to stay in Divine Communion with God.*

*I recently received a letter from a dear lady who asked the question, "How does God want me to prepare?" She says she doesn't fear dying any more, but she wants to carry out her purpose/ agreement with her Spirit and God. She asked, "Does God ever reveal it to you again, once you are on your earthwalk?" Well, I think God speaks to each of us in a way that makes it easy for us to understand. Sometimes He speaks through our feelings, urges, gut reactions, and sometimes He speaks through words. I find that many of my messages come through songs. I begin to hum a melody and sometimes I will remember a song . . . words and melody. These songs haunt my mind. I hear them over and over. Then I think about what the words are saying, how is this song answering my question? Some people get their messages from the written word. Other people get flashes of an idea or intuitions.*

*I believe we can't help but do what we came here to do. Many times it takes years to prepare us. And I believe we are here to do many things, and not just one. As long as you are living your life, to the best of your ability, you won't go wrong. If you have the urge to take up something foreign, do it if it feels right. When I look back on my life, I realize that I'd been prepared. All of my life experiences were taking me to the place where I was available, ready, and somewhat willing to do what was asked of me.*

*I needed a loving and supportive husband like Byron. I needed one who had his skills, know-how, persistence, and bravado.* Mary's Message to the World *wouldn't have become a manuscript without his effort. I began to receive the material that became the book two years after we married. Also, I needed to have already raised my family in order to have the time to spend in prayer and receiving messages. I needed to be this age, so that I could have the life experiences in order to understand the many experiences people have. I needed to be down, in order to appreciate my up times. I needed to know what it is not to love oneself, so that I could go through the task of learning to love myself, so I would be able to encourage you to learn to love yourself. For a few years, I needed to live my life in strife, so that I can appreciate the peaceful life I have now.*

*Another question this lady asked, "How do you know if you are keeping up the commitment?" As long as you are living each day to the fullest, doing what you feel you need to do, being loving and peaceful—you are keeping your commitment. Sometimes we think that being loving is being mushy or slurpy sweet. Now that I love myself, and appreciate that God is in everyone, I don't have the need to fix people. I don't need to overextend myself to be loving. I understand that the most loving thing I can do for people is pray with them. God works so much better than I can. Now that I'm no longer co-dependent, I don't feel the need to rescue anyone. I will help where I can, but I don't give my whole self away trying to make things right or good for others. I know that God gave each person the ability and tools to live this life in unconditional love and with true inner peace.*

*This same lady says she gets frustrated because she shares this information with her family and friends, and they are not receptive. My belief is that this is not about evangelizing or changing anyone else's beliefs. It's about changing ourselves. In Mother Mary's words, it's about "Cleansing our hearts and minds of fear and anger." I think we are to share where Spirit leads us to share, respecting people's beliefs. My lady friend said she is afraid her family and friends will die without being ready.*

*We can't know what is in the heart of others. It isn't up to us to make that judgment. We are required to love God, ourselves, and others without judgment, reservation, or limit. We are urged to be at peace. God is in charge of this world and He is doing a great job of it. Besides, our family and friends may already be ready, we don't know. And if they are not ready, our example and prayers do more good than our words.*

*So hang in there folks, let's pray more and pray regularly for ourselves, our loved ones, and our world. Until next time, I remain your friend, —annie*

✧ ✧ ✧

My Dear Children, I come with a heart filled with love. I urge you to be faithful in your prayers. To be true to yourself. To uphold the tenets of your faith. It is important for you to pray. Yet, prayer without faith is wasted effort. Believe in yourself, believe in the goodness and love of God. Believe that your prayers are answered.

Pray with your whole heart, your entire mind, and your individual soul. Pray as you never have before. Your collective prayers affect great changes in the world. There are many troubled areas in the world, which need the prayers of the faithful to bring calmness, sanity, and a spirit of harmony. You are important to the world, and your prayers are more so. Pray, believing that sanity and harmony can come to people.

Let your words be uplifting, your prayers rise in hope and faith. Keep hope in your heart at all times. Use affirmations of faith to uplift your mind. Remember that my son, Jesus, often asked people who came to him for help, "Do you believe I can do this?" I would have you ask a similar question before you pray. Do you believe God can do this? Do you pray believing that God can help? Do you pray with faith? Faith is very important to the outcome of your prayers.

Speak to God in your own words, or the words of a written prayer used in your religion. Pray the rosary if this is right for you. Pray as you work and as you go about your day. You can use every minute for prayer. Speak from your heart, mind, and soul. You can talk to God about anything. He is an integral part of this world. He is in the mountains, oceans, and He is in you.

The beauty of prayer is that it opens you inner life to the riches of heaven, while you are on earth. Prayer gives your life substance, purpose, and helps you maintain hope in all circumstances and situations. Pray with a grateful heart. Be thankful for all things: life, food, shelter, family, work, opportunities, and for your own Divine connection to God. There is so much to be grateful for.

Prayer, my children, is more than the asking for things. It is the deep communion with God. In this deepest part of your inner life speak to God about your concerns. Empty your heart and mind of all that bothers, confuses, and agitates you. Then you are ready to pray for others. It is not selfish to pray for yourself first. When you empty your heart of your concerns and worries, you are then ready to give your total attention and concentration to others and their concerns.

When you pray for others, release the outcome to God. It is not important for you to know the situation or the circumstance. God knows what is taking place in that person's life. What is important is that you uplift that person with your faith. As you pray with people, you add your prayers to theirs; this allows an inner shift to take place that brings answers, solutions, and rewards. Do not get embroiled in what is happening in the life of the people you pray for. It is not up to you to decide what they need, or what they should have. Simply pray for their highest good, for the best outcome for all concerned. The outcome is between God and the individual. When someone is ill, or downhearted, pray an uplifting prayer of faith. When people are dying, pray for the person and their family. Pray for all people involved in conflict. Pray for both sides of a war, pray for all people affected by the war, no matter what their belief.

Do not say, "This is so hopeless." When you express such sentiments, you greatly dilute your prayers. Say instead, "Let us pray with great hope, knowing that with God all things are possible." This type of statement uplifts, brings healing, and allows for peace and joy to enter the situation. Set your judgments aside. Only judge those situations that affect you directly and require you to make choices. Then make your choices known to God through prayer.

You may say to God, "My loved one is hurting and I would like to see all the pain removed," with the understanding that what is best for your loved one is what God provides. The judgment I speak of is the one that sets you up as a jury, issuing statements of right or wrong. When you pray with this type of judgmental attitude, it is easy to place blame, to want a punishment to take place. Let God judge. He is so much more capable of seeing all hearts, of hearing all the concerns, and of understanding all things.

Often the best prayer is the one that holds the thought of faith for the person who has lost his faith. You can hold the thought of love, for the person who is angry or fearful. You can hold the idea of peace, for those embroiled in family wars. You can hold the feeling of joy for those who live in sadness. You can hold the concept of wholeness for the sick. You can maintain an attitude and a life of faith for yourself, your loved ones and your world.

Believe with your whole heart, intellect, and soul. Peace is possible in the world. It is possible for all lands and all people to live together in harmony. Business and governments can coexist in cooperation with the people. Believe that all things come together for the greatest good of all people. Believe in the Goodness of God and in the goodness of mankind.

Leave all results to God. Only He knows what is truly needed in every situation and in all circumstances. Surrender your prayers and the outcome of your prayers with a faithful and hopeful heart. Let your soul rejoice in the positive outcome before it is seen. Rejoice in answered prayer before you see any sign of the answer. Keep an uplifted attitude and happy countenance. Let your love shine through your faith. Love God with your whole faith, your whole joy, and your hopeful heart. This is how to pray. This is how to maintain an attitude of prayer and faith. Set aside your doom and gloom. It has no place in a faithful soul. Put away your woes and your tales of heartache; there is no room in the faithful heart for this.

My children, in all your prayers keep hope in your heart, faith in your life, and peace in your every thought. You can affect great changes in the days to come. You can start a great surge of peace on earth and goodwill towards all men. I have faith in you and in your prayers.

Mary, Mother of Jesus.

# Seek God's Solace

4/98

RECENTLY, I'VE HAD SOME VERY SHOCKING REVELATIONS *about myself. I've known I needed to learn self-discipline and I was aware I had not paid attention to my body. But what I didn't know was the extent to which I had been denying my physical body. I've not paid attention to it throughout my whole life. So to begin to be concerned about my body at this late date is quite a feat of self-discipline. The day I received the diagnosis of diabetes, I asked, what is my lesson in this? The answer came quickly—self-discipline. It didn't surprise me. But I felt like I was facing something I'd been avoiding for many years, not just in this life experience either. Oh, I took care to look as neat as I could, but then I'd forget all about myself.*

*Over the last year and a half, I've been good about the diet part of this program. What I'm realizing is that I'm back to my old lesson in acceptance. It's another opportunity to work with the Prayer of Serenity. You know, accept what can't be changed and change what can. My dilemma has been to ask, what can be changed? Yes, I believe with my whole heart that with God all things are possible. I believe I can have an instantaneous healing. But there has been something nagging at me. For months I thought I needed to go through this experience, or that it was my choice to work some things out this way. So back to my question what can be changed, and what can't?*

## SEEK GOD'S SOLACE

*My body and its needs has been something I've not wanted to think about. I've acted a lot like Scarlett O'Hara, "I'll think about it tomorrow." But tomorrow never came. For years it was easier not to think about it; there was so much I needed to attend to, children, husband, mother, friends, work, later my emotional healing, my spiritual growth, and just about anything that enabled me to avoid the subject. I really worked at running away from the need to care for my body. I've done such a good job of ignoring my body that even today, I don't know when I'm in pain. Byron will look at my expression, hear my crankiness, and tell me I'm hurting. It seems ridiculous to deny your body to this extent.*

*Self-discipline is the pits, but then learning to love myself felt the same way. It's a struggle. I keep hearing my therapist saying, "Stay in the struggle, Annie." So I am staying in the struggle, watching my food intake, and all the rest that goes with caring for myself with this ailment.*

*So my lesson is self-discipline. Just what is self-discipline anyway? Often the messages that come from my readings say that discipline is teaching. It also could be training and practice. I'm teaching myself new eating habits and training myself to live healthy and honor this body. I've found many erroneous beliefs still deep within me. My inner guidance says there is still some residue of the belief that in order to serve God I need to suffer. Well, that's one belief that is no longer true of my conscious mind. It's time to eliminate it from my subconscious mind.*

*In the messages that became* Mary's Message to the World, *Mother Mary said She was as concerned about our physical life as our spiritual. That we were to prepare both physically and spiritually. In these last ten years I've concentrated on the spiritual, emotional, and mental parts of me. But to be whole while on earth the physical is important too. I'm down to preparing my body for whatever the future brings.*

*I don't know where this is going, or what point I'm trying to make except to say that when we go into denial, sooner or later we must face ourselves. Another point could be that one aspect of our being isn't more important than the other. To be whole means that every part of ourself must be as good as the rest. One other thing has been coming to mind: this process is just another step in loving myself. When we love ourselves totally, we care and tend to every aspect of our life: body, mind, and soul.*

*I don't know if I will accomplish the goal I've set for my physical body. But with my doctor's help, I'm sure going to give it my all, and let the end results rest in God's hands. Who knows, it could easily be much better than I hoped for. Just maybe if I do my best to correct my thoughts and actions concerning the care of my body, and if I pray and meditate on this, I will be healthier than I've been in years. I know for sure that God loves me more than I can understand. It's His good pleasure to give us life and to give it to us abundantly. My lessons in self discipline are becoming numerous. But then, aren't all our lessons this way. Don't we learn much more than we thought we would in the beginning?*

*Well, folks thank you for letting me share some very personal thoughts. You are so good this way. I appreciate you. Until next time, I remain your friend, —annie*

◆ ◆ ◆

MY DEAR CHILDREN, I come to bring you solace. A word of cheer, comfort, and love as you go through the trials and tribulations of the great change. To the human heart change is frightening and upsetting. When you rely on the Divine Creator, you are guided to the right place, people, and situations which will help you in the moment. Begin today, if you haven't already, to live in the moment. Let your thoughts for the future be of good cheer and hope. Plan for the future in your own way, take whatever action you are guided to, and then live in the moment. This moment is yours . . . it is Divine. Let your plans and actions fill you with solace.

Let solace comfort your soul, bring cheer to your heart, and relief to your anxieties. The soul is comforted through prayer and meditation. Keep to your daily prayers. Bring to God all the things in your life that cause you concern. Pray for your life, omitting no area of your existence. Do not think that you can hide from God. Speak to Him about everything. Are there situations which fail you? Are there areas in your world that concern you? Are you troubled about loved ones? Do you fret over a particular situation? God sees everything and knows everything, yet you cannot benefit until you open yourself up to His help and loving solutions. Keep nothing hidden in your heart or mind. Release your concerns, worries, and problems to God. Let Him bring solace by giving you insights into solutions and answers. Allow God to move circumstances and situations to answer your prayers and petitions.

My children, set aside a time to listen through your meditations. During your meditations commune with God. Commune with Him in silence. Be still and let the silence soothe your soul. Simply allow your meditations to become a vigil in silence. In the beginning you may find it difficult to maintain silence, but with practice you will become more proficient. You may only be able to maintain silence for a few seconds or minutes, that is good. Continue to be in the silence no matter how long you can maintain it. Do not judge what happens in the silence. The silence, which is your interaction with all that is Divine, cannot be judged or measured on earth. In time you will become more comfortable in the silence. Your heart will begin to rejoice and you will experience relief which is felt to the core of your being. When you are weary or troubled, seek solace in the silence of your soul. When you are sad and grieving, seek the solace of silence. When you are confused and questioning, seek the solace of silence. When you are joyous and grateful, seek the communion with God in silence.

Allow yourself to find solace in the joys of your life. The Psalmist said, "Make a joyful noise unto the Lord." This is the way to worship God. He loves you unconditionally and this brings comfort and joy to the soul. Daily find the joy in living. Look for ways to be cheerful and have goodwill. When you concentrate on the joys of your life, you become more grateful, more compassionate, and much more understanding. While you are on earth, there will be troubles, but leave your troubles in the silence and allow God to work miracles. Concentrate on the joys of life and not on the troubles of life.

We can say over and over, "Do not judge, for how you judge others is how you are judged." But until you find the solace of God, you will continue to fall into old patterns of judgment. God's solace brings relief through forgiveness. Until you can fully accept that you are loved unconditionally, forgiven completely for all things, you will continue to fall into judgment. And until you can forgive yourself for all things, both imagined and real, you will not find the comfort that comes from a soul at peace.

Forgive yourself for all your mistakes, sins, errors in judgment, and for anything that distresses you. Some people have great things to forgive, such as crimes and abuses of all kinds. Others must forgive themselves for being unkind, dispassionate, and uninvolved in their own life and in the lives of their loved ones. Forgive yourself for the large issues and for the small annoyances. Then you receive God's great solace. Through His solace, He brings relief from these issues and annoyances, and gives comfort in the awareness of inner peace. His forgiveness is soothing to the spirit. Your own forgiveness frees you from living in inner terror.

## SEEK GOD'S SOLACE

Now you are ready to forgive others. To free yourself and the people you have issues with from all entanglements of the soul. This brings you more solace than you can imagine. You then are free to be cheerful, to live a life of peaceful joy. This is your goal, this is your possibility. As you forgive all people and all things, you are helping to bring peace into your life and into the world.

Seek to experience joyful peace, the peace that passes all understanding. My children, you were created to live in peace, believe this with your whole heart. Let this thought and the knowledge that you are loved unconditionally, lead you to truly experience joyful peace.

First find peace within yourself. Commit to live your life in peace; this is how to help bring peace into the world. There is solace in making this commitment. It gives you comfort and it will also bring up all the issues that keep you from peace. But do not let this deter you from your goal of inner peace. Recognize that these issues are to be forgiven, released, and resolved, in order for you to live in peace. Each of you have all that you need within you to accomplish this task.

Then live your life joyfully. Find the joy in everyday life, in doing your work well. Find the joy in relating to your family and friends. Seek to know yourself. Find the joy and humor that is a part of your spirit. Daily seek to be of good cheer. Not ignoring problems, but resolving them with grace. There is joy in every sunset and sunrise, in nature and in your children. Find the joy in your pursuits and your hobbies. Find the joy of being a good example for others to follow. Find the joy in prayer and meditation. This is my request. I do not request the impossible of you. Each of you has the capacity to find solace, to live in peace, and to live joyfully. Let your daily life be loving, cheerful, and soothing to humanity. Your daily life then becomes the joyful noise you make to God. Let your life reflect God's love.

Mary, Mother of Jesus.

# 40

## Each Day Is a Gift

6/98

*"As I live and learn."* This phrase seems to be my watchword. I certainly am living and learning. I'm still working with the same lesson; how to listen to my body, or maybe it's becoming aware of my body. Now is the time for me to heal the body and it's carrying as much old baggage as my heart and mind did . . . combined.

But first, I want to take this time to thank the many people who have come through my life with all kinds of healing modalities. Many of you have offered to provide me with the herbs, tonics, or other products that have helped you or your clients to heal. I haven't been able to stay with any one program because of my own lack of attention. I really, really appreciate your kind thoughts, good-will, and love. Over the years I've received countless massages, Reiki treatments, and other forms of body and energy work, with good results. I am improving. Like everything else in life, it flows like the tides. I have good days and some that are not so good. Now I have more good days than not.

I'm working with the prayer of serenity on this. One place I lack discipline is in exercise. I don't like to exercise even though I know the importance of it. So my prayer is that I have the courage, fortitude, and motivation to stay with an exercise program. I've started doing this so many times, that I could say, I'm the queen of start-ups. It's the stick-to-it-ness that I need. Maybe I'll quit starting and just consider the lapses as my normal way of exercising. Then I will be on the same program. Something happens when we start over and over. At least, it does for me. I begin to feel like a failure. I can easily become defeated. I'm remembering Mother Mary's admonition to "Live Her message, as best I can." Maybe that's the key to working on our individual lessons. Maybe we just keep working everyday to the best of our own ability.

Many people are working out their life issues through health, wealth, or relationships. It doesn't matter what we are facing, if we will just do our best each day. Then stop judging what our best is. If we compare our best today with our best of yesterday, or last week, we'll find discrepancies. What I found, when I was learning to love myself, was that I couldn't judge one days best with a past best. Yesterday my best may have been that I could work in the yard, or walk through a mall all afternoon. If today my best is that I can only get out of bed and care for my personal needs, then that's my best. Maybe what's most important is that we keep on, keeping on. That is the piece that I've lacked and am learning now.

When I was learning to love myself unconditionally, I learned not to judge my day. I learned to be happy with what I could do, not to look back to last week, or a year ago. So many times people bemoan the fact that they can't do as much as they used to. This is especially true as we age. To constantly be looking back, as a measure of our potential, is to limit ourselves to the past. But to be constantly looking forward, to a future that is at best only a dream, is to live outside of oneself. It's the "NOW" that is important. It's what we are doing today that counts, not what we did yesterday, or what we want to do tomorrow. I'm using the phrase, "Now is the time," as an affirmation. I've wasted many days ignoring my own life, thoughts, body, and spirit. I don't intend to waste anymore days.

Another thing I'm learning is that God intended for us to enjoy life. This is done easier when we set our judgments aside. He loves each of us, unconditionally, and wants us to enjoy our human experience. One of the first things I heard, as I began to listen to my inner guidance was, "Lighten up, get the pun, Annie?" At the time I *was concerned with my weight. I'm learning to see the humor in every situation, no matter how dire, or devastating it appears. It's not that we're going to live life without problems. We're going to live life with the ability to honestly see and face our problems with God's help: we can resolve anything, face anything, and we can be content with ourselves and our lives. I don't believe that in order to be spiritual, my life must be perfect. Too many times people are disappointed if things don't go well. They look at their life with the thought that, this is good and this is bad. I no longer see my life in those terms. I know that everything is good when I concentrate on God and His love. My greatest lessons have begun as tragedies. I've learned that it isn't important for my life to be perfect, because, with God, I can handle anything in love, peace, and with humor.*

*I'm learning to appreciate and accept my body, with all its quirks and faults. Many times it's our attitude that counts, and may need changing. As you can tell, I take what is happening in my life and use it to learn my spiritual lessons. I was taught to do this by The Brotherhood and Mother Mary. She once said to me, about my son's past drinking problem, "We'll take care of the inside and when the inside is right, the outside will take care of itself." So one of my lessons is self-discipline, I'm becoming more disciplined in my meditations. I'm given nudges, ideas, and insights on what I need to do. Now I have hope and faith that I will keep on getting better, and better, and better.*

*Until next time I remain, your friend, —annie*

◇ ◇ ◇

M<small>Y</small> D<small>EAR</small> C<small>HILDREN</small>, I come to you in peace and with a great love in my heart. We are one, because we are one with God, our Creator. We are united in love, peace, and joy. I would have you live your life free of all lingering fears, all unresolved angers, and all impediments to your good. You have all the tools, all the capabilities to live your life in love, peace, and joy today.

Begin your day with a grateful heart. Begin each day with a prayer of thanksgiving. When you think of your day, remember, it's a gift. Decide to live it to its fullest. Let your morning be one of inner preparation as you prepare yourself for work, or play, or whatever is on your agenda for that particular day. Each morning commit to live this one day in peace. Let love rule your thoughts, and let joy be your goal.

You can do this. You begin with yourself and then expand your circle to include your family, then your fellowman. Begin with small acts of courtesy. Let your love show as you acknowledge people as fellow humans in this life. Smile more, allow others to see your joy. It matters not if they return your smile. You are not smiling to gather a basket of smiles. You are smiling to demonstrate your joy for life, your peaceful heart and your goodwill. Let yourself smile as a token of your love for God's love.

You can be peaceful, if you will determine to resolve all old angers. If you will forgive quickly, you can live in peace when you fail to take offense. You can be peaceful, when you decide, commit, and do all you can to live in peace. This does not mean you will never become angry. It means that when you do become angry, you will quickly begin to find ways to disperse your anger in healthy ways. Never cause injury to anyone or to yourself. Anger is a part of your make-up, placed deep within you for a good reason. It is the same reason you have been imbued with fear. Anger and fear are a means to protect yourself. These emotions become detrimental to your health and peace when they are harbored, and when you refuse to address them.

Remember that anger and fear were given to you for a reason. They are held deep within you to protect you, either by giving you the energy to flee, or to fight, when you are in danger. They have their good uses. It was never intended for you to use these powerful emotions to harm yourself or others. It was never intended for you to keep these emotions locked away in your heart and mind. These emotions were placed within you to be used for a short period of time. Then you were to return to your natural state of contentment, love, and peace.

Any fear held within your heart for days, has been held too long. Any anger or resentment that you have held for longer than a few days has been held too long. Do everything that you can, when you can, to eliminate these lingering fears and all unresolved angers. This is imperative as you enter this new era. It is imperative that you become peaceful. It is imperative that you love unconditionally. It is important that you become joyful. Enjoy every experience and seek the good that is within every situation and every circumstance. Through your seeking, you grow, and through the search you travel the path to spirituality and peace. The journey to peace is an important one. You need to travel the entire way. Seek to eliminate these emotions from your heart of hearts. It is through the settling of difference and the forgiving of mistakes, that you come close to God. Cry the tears that wash away the pain of unresolved angers. Scream the hurts out of your heart and mind. Speak the words that will eliminate these depleting emotions from within you. But cry, scream, and speak these emotions, out of you, in a healthy way. It is not healthy to scream words that will cause harm or pain to your loved ones. It is not healthy to berate yourself for mistakes of the past.

It is healthy to speak, cry, or scream your pain, tears, and words in prayer. It is healthy to ask God to help you resolve all depleting emotions.

You can do this, my children. You will be guided to the method, people, and organizations that will help you the most. Not everyone can do this without the help of doctors, spiritual leaders, or counselors. It is not incorrect to ask for help. It is a good way to become peaceful. I have complete faith and trust in your inner abilities. Do this now. Become peaceful.

Then you are ready to love in joyful peace. It is the peace that passes all understanding. You are ready to be called children of peace. Jesus said, "Blessed are the peacemakers for they will be called children of God" (Matthew 5:9). This is you. Jesus was speaking of you today. You have the opportunity to usher in peace through the settling of angry resentments and lingering fears. You can be peaceful when you live to forgive all things. When you live in a state of natural forgiveness you will not take offense, but be instantly at peace by forgiving all things, at all times, and with all people.

You can be joyful. You have all the capabilities of living in peace. You have the inner ability to live in joy. Enjoy life and enjoy life as you live it today. Enjoy your home and enjoy your family. Take pleasure in the little things in life. Take pleasure in a beautiful sky, the stars, and the moon. Take pleasure in your talents. Seek to find your creativity. Everyone has these abilities. Your talents may not be like anyone else but you have talents.

Find the joy of prayer and meditation. Concentrate on the good in your life. Seek to expand that good through your joy. Let yourself enjoy breathing, eating, sleeping, working, and playing. Let yourself see the good in others. Welcome the joys of nature. Take pleasure in the sunset and the dawning of a new day. Find something to enjoy each day. It maybe a huge thing like the birth of a child, or the visit of loved ones, or a wedding. It may be in the simple things of life, like the enjoyment of doing chores. Everything in life can be enjoyed, if you have the right attitude and seek the joy in every situation. When you cry, enjoy your tears. When you laugh, enjoy the humor. When you play, enjoy the game. This is how to live in joyful peace. You can do this, my children. I know you can.

Remember always, that I am loving you as God does, without condition and without limit.

Mary, Mother of Jesus.

# Live in Joy

8/98

*I'M GETTING BETTER AND BETTER ALL THE TIME. My health/energy still ebbs and flows. In the last few months I've dealt more with the psychological adjustments than the physical. Long before Mother Mary began to come to me, I'd prayed for a healing of body, mind, and soul. I've been healing the long-held emotional and mental angers and fears. Now it's time to heal the body. I don't think my soul ever needed healing because it's the part of me that retains my original pattern. In my original state I am perfect, just as you are. But to access that state, I've had to let go of a lot of junk and garbage such as: resentments, phobias, fear, rage, shame, guilt, pride, and co-dependency.*

*It sounds like I've arrived and don't have these issues anymore. In reality, they still rear their ugly head from time to time, causing me to feel "bad." I no longer rage, but I do get angry. I no longer have phobias, but I can become fearful. Now that I've experienced the peace and joy of living without the "bad feelings," I can more easily let go of them when they do arise in my life. Thank you for your continual prayers; they are helping me tremendously. I count your prayers as one of my greatest blessings.*

*There are times I'm ashamed of my physical ailments. As you see, I'm not completely done with my shame issues. The shame of illness happens more often when I'm around people who think that* having an ailment is not spiritual. They think that being spiritual means a magical life without pain or need of any kind. My intent is not to discount their belief. If that is how their spirituality is experienced, then I say "more power to them." I asked to be healed in body, mind, and soul, so it's taking me longer. I'm now clearing away issues that have been with me through hundreds of years. It's more important to rid myself of this old garbage than to look spiritual.

Sherry Hansen Steiger sent me a copy of her new book, The Power of Prayer to Heal and Transform Your Life. She includes a prayer that is often listed as "source unknown." Sherry says it's one of her favorite prayers, and she has seen it attributed to St. Francis.

### I Asked God

*I asked God for strength, that I might achieve.*
*I was made weak, that I might learn to obey.*
*I asked God for health, that I might do great things.*
*I was given infirmity, that I might do better things.*
*I asked God for riches, that I might be happy.*
*I was given poverty, that I might be wise.*
*I asked God for power, that I might have approval.*
*I was given weakness, that I might feel the need for God.*
*I asked for all things, that I might enjoy life.*
*I was given life, that I might enjoy all things.*
*I got nothing that I asked for, but everything I hoped for,*
*I am among all people, most richly blessed!*

—St. Francis

I highly recommend Sherry Steiger's book. She tells wonderful stories of real-life cases. Plus, she gives her views on how to teach your children to pray. It helped remind me of how many ways prayer helps us.

I recently watched an HBO Special titled, "The Innocent Ones." If you have the opportunity . . . watch it. You too will be moved to do more for the children of the world. It's a documentary about the difficulties children in different countries live in, in order to survive. Not only is poverty highlighted, but abuse. There are young girls in Africa who are given to a tribal priest as tribal virgins to become slaves for their religions. These girls live their entire lives in slavery in the homes of the priest. In Africa and Asia many children are sold into slavery. They work from before dawn to after dark all of their lives, without pay, or anyone to care.

The film showed street children in Central America who are addicted to glue. This is the glue that has been banned here in America. In film clips you saw how children are treated in orphanages and mental institutions. In many countries around the world children who are mentally retarded and have cerebral palsy are locked away, for life. I have a son who is mentally retarded, and this really touched me in a very sensitive spot. Also shown were children in many nations who become prostitutes because that is the only way they can earn a living. And still, they live in such poverty it is heart-wrenching. My heart went out to the children. They represented thousands of children world wide. The documentary didn't exclude any continent. It showed the dire and sad ways children live here in our own USA.

I remember Mother Mary's admonition to pray for Her children as I watched this. I also remember Her saying that the first thing we should do for our loved ones is to pray for them, because it was the best we could offer. My heart has been in prayer since I watched this film. What great changes we can make in children's lives around the world, if we pray for them, daily. Join me in praying for the children of the world. Remember, it's the best thing we can do. I believe in the power of prayer to change things that can be changed. Abuse, addiction, and ignorance certainly can be changed. Children need our prayers. In the film clips, the children looked hopeless, lost, and unloved.

We can make a difference in our world. Often we think there is nothing we can do, but each of us can pray. We can send our love to all children, and into the trouble spots on our planet. Please don't forget the children. Until next time, I remain your friend, who sends you love. —annie

✧ ✧ ✧

## LIVE IN JOY

My Dear Children, I come to you in joy and a heart filled with love. It is through God's love that I am with you. It is because He is love that we are one. His love is the means of communication which allows us to join our spirits in joy and peace.

Daily seek to live in joy. There is a sense of joy nestled within life; do all you can to find it. There is peace you can experience as you live your life in God's love. It is God's life force that animates you daily. He is closer than your breath, your heartbeat, or your thoughts. He is more alive than you and more loving than you can imagine. Live to enjoy your life. Enjoy your work, your family, and your life issues. Enjoy all phases of your life. Do not decry any part of your life, because it is through the experience of living that you are alive. Many times you are more alive in times of distress.

If for any reason you are not enjoying your life, then seek to find what negates your joy. When you find the issues that keep you from experiencing joy, do all you can to release them, forgive them, and let them all go. Let nothing interfere in your joyful, peaceful existence.

You can bring more joy into your life through your prayers and meditations. As you concentrate on joy, you may notice the situations and circumstances in your life that are not joyous. You may first become aware of the experiences that need to be released and forgiven. Forgive, my children, for through forgiveness you are guided into more peace and joy than you had before experienced. I am asking you to find the peace that passes all understanding.

Rejoice, for you are loved; you are filled with a life force that allows you to make your own choices. Rejoice that you are capable of experiencing. Be grateful and rejoice that you can love, that you can become peaceful. Rejoice in your communications with God. Rejoice that you are filled with His spirit. Rejoice that you are alive. Let your whole life be a reflection of the joy that God has in you. Let your whole being reflect the love that God has for you.

Now my children, pray that you may be of service to Him. Let God guide you in ways to express your joy. Let God take you by the hand and lead you in ways of exhibiting His great love. There are many ways to express your joyful, peaceful, loving nature. You can demonstrate God's love in your life, through your compassion, kindness, and caring. There are many ways to do this. You can bring kindness and caring into neglectful situations. You can deal with people with compassion and understanding. You can show God's love in your life by caring for yourself and your loved ones without judgment. You can demonstrate your caring by helping the downtrodden, hungry, and the elderly. But most of all you can express your joy and love through your prayers for all people regardless of religion, race, culture, or nationality.

In angry or warring situations you can bring an element of peace through your understanding and tolerance. Where there is strife, let your peace bring a voice of reason. Where there is anger, let your whole being reflect God's peace. Let your words, thoughts, and deeds serve to enhance instead of deter. Let your prayers rise up in love. Be quick to forgive all that is hurtful or cruel. Be the first to forgive, the first to understand, and the first to return all situations to a peaceful state.

Let your joy reflect in your ability to see the humor in all situations. Let your joy infect others with pleasure. In strife filled circumstances, do not become caught up in the strife, but look for the joy, the good, the blessing in that eventuality.

## LIVE IN JOY

When you can maintain your joy in times of strife, you will go a long way towards promoting peace. When you can help others to have fun, you will be working for peace. When you can shed pleasure in people's life, you are being loving as God is.

Give people the opportunity to laugh and to find the joy in their lives. Many times people become too serious in their lives. They forget to enjoy the common things. There is joy in rising early to watch a sunrise. There is joy in talking or playing with children. There is joy in admiring nature. Enjoy your locality. Let yourself enjoy the deserts, the seashores, the meadows, the woodlands, and the marshes. Let yourself find pleasure in the birds, and small creatures of God. Let yourself find the pleasure of a simple conversation. Help your neighbor in any way you can, and let your neighbor help you.

Seriously seek to find God within you and within your life. Then seriously have fun as you work, as you care for your loved ones, and as you go about your daily task. Become joyful in your entire being. Let your joy be in having a good, sturdy connection to God. Let your pleasure be in having dialogue with God. Let joy enhance your workday. Let peace be your priority. Let love be how you live your life. Do all you can, in your own way, to become joyful peacemakers on earth now.

Jesus said, "Blessed are the peacemakers, for they shall be called children of God." You are already God's child; now become peaceful, so that you can be the peacemaker. Take stock of your life. Ferret out all those resentments, envies, animosities, indignation, fears, phobias, and any depleting emotion. Do not let any bitterness of past events deter you from experiencing peace, love, or joy. In order for you to become a peacemaker, you must first cleanse your heart and mind of all depleting emotions, all contrary thought patterns, and all strife in your life. When you have done this, you become not only peaceful but joyful and more loving than you have ever been.

As the Psalmist said, "Make a joyful noise unto the Lord." He also said, "Serve God with gladness." You too can serve God with gladness and with love. Serve God by doing all you can to become the peaceful, joyful, loving person you were created to be. You can do this, my children. I am sure that you have all the capabilities, the know-how and the means to become a joyful, loving, and peaceful person. You can reflect God's love in your locality. You can be instrumental in living your life in peaceful, joyful ways. You teach more by example than with your words. Let your life be the means you teach others to find their truth, their peace, and their joy.

Remember always that I am loving you and praying with you. You are dear, you are wonderful, you are my child, whom I love.

Mary, Mother of Jesus.

# Be Grateful for Your Blessings

10/98

*I* GOOFED*! To everyone who received empty newsletters in August, I apologize for the inconvenience. I was trying to do it all myself and it just didn't work. It's really funny, how from our goofs we can learn. We received the newsletter from the printer on Wednesday afternoon before our August 15th openhouse. I didn't think it would be a problem. Byron couldn't help because the phone was ringing off the wall. He asked if I had anyone to help, but I thought I could do it myself. Well my pride and ego took over and as always . . . pride goes before a fall. I thought, just wait until Byron sees that I can do all of this perfectly, ha-ha. At the time, we were having a new floor covering installed in the bathrooms. As always, one thing gets done, and another gets undone. Then we had to have the plumber out to repair the damage done while installing the new floor. Through all of the interruptions and questions, I'm stuffing envelopes, getting them ready for mailing. I sent out somewhere between 50 to 60 empty newsletter envelopes.*

*The next Monday the phone calls began to come in asking for a newsletter because there wasn't one in their pretty pink envelopes. You have a wonderful sense of humor. Everyone was so very nice and polite about it. Most people blamed the post office. It wasn't the post office who goofed, but me. Once again, please forgive me. I will ask for help in the future and not try to do everything myself. Talk about instant karma! I thought I'd show Byron how much better I am at sending out the newsletter than he is, and Spirit knocks me off my high-horse. I really enjoyed the letters from you to ask that another newsletter be sent. If you are wondering where Byron was, he was answering the phone, giving directions, taking orders, and getting the B&A building ready for visitors.*

*Asking for help and letting someone know what I need is one of the things I've been working on for years. I thought I'd already learned it, but evidently I haven't, since it has been so blatantly revealed to me that I've not completely learned this lesson. It's time for me to take my inventory once again. Could it be that I'm not asking for what I need through my prayers? Most likely this is true. Mother Mary said that because, we have freedom of choice, God awaits our voicing our request and needs before He answers.*

*I usually get into trouble when I fail to ask for help. It's not that I think I'm so wonderful or smart. It's more that I don't want to disturb or impose on people. But then, maybe this goes back to the issue of self-worth. I have to look at this more. Once again, thank you for being so understanding and so very humorous in asking for your newsletter.*

*On August 15th, Mother Mary has made an apparition yearly since 1992. We have been directed to be near water at sunset. Our meeting place now is Lake Tenkiller near our home. It was a very mystical experience. This year an eight-year-old girl saw Mother Mary in physical form standing on the lake. Mother Mary talked to her and gave her five messages, some were personal. Mother Mary asked the little girl to pray for all the people living near seashores because bad things were going to happen. Our little friend says that Mother Mary also asked us to pray for peace.*

*I too received five requests from Mother Mary during the time the sun was spinning and changing colors. First, She asked us to pray for all children, the ones who are living in violence and the ones who have loving homes. Second, we are to pray for all teenagers, because these are difficult and confusing times for them. Again the request was for all, no matter if their home situations were unloving or loving. Third, we are to pray for all families in the world. She specifically asked that we pray for an end to all family wars, feuds, and quarrels. Fourth, She asked us to pray for humanity. Through our prayers we can change the race consciousness. Fifth, She asked us to pray for peace: for peace to come into the hearts of all people, peace to be a reality in families, peace in our institutions, and peace in the world.*

*As we have done every year after the sun sinks over the horizon, we gather into a circle and if I've received any messages, I share them. We close our evening singing "Amazing Grace" and "Let there Be Peace on Earth." Every year has been different and yet every year has been the same. Each year the sun has spun and changed colors. Often there have been blue globes of light around the sun. The second year and this year, little girls have seen Mother Mary. The second year, (1992), two little sisters saw Mother Mary in the sky. This year one little girl saw Her standing on the water. Most people who attended have felt Mary's presence and felt the love and peace which has been a part of each apparition.*

*Several people said they felt like everyone who attended were in reality a family. Many years ago The Brotherhood asked us to open our home and family meditations to the rest of our family. So it's not surprising that we feel the family connection. We are a family. We are the human family, so I guess it's time to begin to love our family, set aside our prejudices, and to love our family unconditionally. It's simple, but not easy. I have no doubt we can all do our part. It was a wonderful weekend and Mother Mary made it all special.*

*Check our website for more information on August 15 at: http://www.baproducts.com/marydy98.htm —annie*

◇ ◇ ◇

M<small>Y</small> D<small>EAR</small> C<small>HILDREN</small>, I come to you in love. Today I request that you remember who you are. Each of you is the beloved child of a benevolent Creator. Find the many blessings which make up your life. Be grateful for each of these blessings.

You are blessed with life, a life that is ever flowing, ever changing, and ever yours. You are in charge of your life. God has blessed you with the freedom to always choose to live your life as you like. If you think you are not living your life as you like, then find out why. What is missing in your life, what can be improved? What can you do today to improve your life? Remember that life is lived from the inside out. Focus on your inner life: what you think, what your thought patterns are, and what your behavior patterns are choosing for you. How you think, is how you choose to live. Your thought patterns are the guidelines for your choices. Your behavior patterns will demonstrate to you how you think in your inner core. These are blessings, my children. The blessing of seeing for yourself where you are headed. And . . . the blessing of changing your life, by changing your attitudes, thoughts, behavior patterns, and beliefs.

You are blessed with the capacity to love and to be loved. All of God's children have this great gift. You experience love in so many ways. There is the love you experience as a little child from your mother, father, siblings, grandparents, and other family members. As you grow in stature you experience the love of friends, teachers, and peers. You begin to understand the workings of love. Then as an adult you experience the love of a mate, companion, and spouse. Throughout your life as you experience love, hopefully you learn to appreciate and accept yourself. When you can love yourself, then you can truly love others. When you become a parent you return to the beginning as you experience the love of your children. To love and be loved is one of the greatest blessings there is, because you experience love as it comes to you and as it goes out from you. Acknowledging God's love by loving unconditionally is the greatest gift you can give yourself and others.

## BE GRATEFUL FOR YOUR BLESSINGS

You are blessed with the capacity to change. You always have the ability to change many things in your life. You can change your attitudes, behavior patterns, and thought patterns. These may not be easy to change alone, but your other blessing is that you do not have to do it alone. There is help. God, the Father, is ever ready to help you if what you desire is for your good and the good of others. This is a wonderful blessing. Because this means you do not have to live in dire circumstances or situations. You can change. When you ask the Father within to help you, you will be led to the people, organizations, and institutions that can help you make the needed changes.

You are blessed with a direct connection to The Source of All Good, who is the Father within. Through this connection you receive guidance. You keep these lines of communication clear through your prayers and meditations. You are never alone, God is always with you. He respects and loves you enough to allow you to call upon Him when you want. Through those times when you neglect this communication, God continues to love you. All you need is to want to be in touch with God and He is there. The help you seek will come to you in amazing and miraculous ways, and through everyday routine ways. God will not let you down. God blesses you with your own inner ability to speak to Him and to hear Him. God is always listening to you.

You are blessed with the ability to forgive. You can forgive when you can let go of depleting emotions. You can forgive and forget to such an extent that the hurt, shame, guilt, or whatever depleting emotion is never remembered. You can forgive yourself. You have this great ability and it is a blessing. As you wipe the slate clean of depleting emotions and situations, then you are free to love unconditionally.

You are blessed with joy. You have the innate ability to experience happiness, pleasure, and mirth. It is within you to take pleasure in the common things: like the sunset, sunrise, forest, and seashores. You can take pleasure in your loved ones, and in their accomplishments, talents, and love. You can take pleasure in your work, career, hobbies, and sports. It is within you to enjoy humor and see the humor in life. You have everything you need to be happy. You lack nothing. If you are not happy today, then look within to find what is keeping you from experiencing joy.

You have the blessing of experiencing peace. You can experience peace when you clear away all the depleting emotions and situations. As you work to clear away the fears and phobias of your life, you become stronger because you can realize more of yourself. Then peace can be a reality in your everyday life. To be peaceful is to be forgiving and you already know you have this ability. To live a life of peace is to accept and love yourself and all people unconditionally. To live a peaceful life is to strengthen and empower humanity to change from its warring ways to a peaceful consciousness.

You are blessed with a beautiful world and wonderful resources. There is so much beauty in this world. There are the changing seasons, great mountains, and rolling hills. There are so many wonderful beaches and seacoasts. There are the many animals who live on this planet with you. There is beauty in daytime and in the night. There is beauty in the minerals and the people of this world. There are so many different kinds of foliage and plants to enhance your existence. You have so much beauty in this world that, wherever you look, you see beauty.

Your greatest blessing is you. You are unique and individual. You are different from any other person on earth. You have many abilities, talents, capacities, powers, and skills. You only need to allow yourself to express all your blessings and all that you are.

All these blessings come with a responsibility to care for yourself, your loved ones, your fellow humans, and your world. Be grateful for all these wonderful blessings. Your main responsibility is to pray, to love, and to live in peace. I request that you stay in an attitude of gratitude, because you are truly blessed and loved.

Mary, Mother of Jesus.

# Promote Peace

12/98

*I HOPE YOU ENJOYED Thanksgiving as much as we did. I'm finding that every day is thanksgiving when you are truly grateful for your blessings. Over the last few years, I've become more and more grateful. Maybe it's an age thing, but I'm grateful just to be alive! When I realize that this is God's life force flowing through me, it's difficult not to be grateful. One of my greatest blessings is you. I so appreciate your continued support. I meet the neatest people as I travel across the country. At times I lose their address. It is very frustrating to want to communicate my appreciation and not be able to. So if any of you are among the people I never sent a thank you to for all your help, it's probably that I lost your address and can't remember your full name. For some reason I can remember entire conversations, describe a person in detail, and not their name. When I've lost, misplaced, or left without a way to communicate with a person, I pray for them, because it is my way of remembering your friendship and caring. Through this newsletter, I send you a heartfelt thank you, for driving me to the airport, picking me up at the airport, and for the many other ways people help.*

*Everyone celebrates Jesus' birth at this time of the year. This year I feel that I'm to celebrate Jesus' life, not just his birth. The Brotherhood and Mother Mary have said that Jesus came to demonstrate our full potential. When people were amazed at the healing that took place through him, Jesus himself said that we could do all the things he did and greater things.*

*Jesus gave us only one commandment. We are to love God with all our heart, all our mind, and all our soul . . . then we are to love our neighbor as ourself. I wonder how frustrated he must be to know that two thousand years later we still are not able to follow that one commandment. Of course I know that Jesus is always loving and patient, because I've had a taste of his love and patience. But still it must be daunting.*

*Often I voice my love to God and tell Him why I love Him. In reality the reasons I love Him are also my blessings. I love God because He is so good to me. Whenever I've needed Him, He has been there for me. I love God for His life force that flows through me and makes me unique and individual. I love God because he gave us such a beautiful world to live in. I love God for my creativity, which is demonstrated through many avenues. I love God because I've been able to reach my first heartfelt wish and goal . . . to be a mother, grandmother, and great-grandmother, and still be young enough to enjoy it. I love God because he answered my prayer for a loving, supportive, and demonstrative husband and life partner.*

*Today I'm able to love God for all of my past experiences, even those that were abusive and hurtful. This was not always the case. I love God because He helped me work through the pain and anger to find a place of inner peace and forgiveness. I love God for my work with Mother Mary. I love God for all the wonderful friends I've made through this work. I love God for my helper/angels, who come disguised as friends, therapist, doctors, and fellow humans.*

*I could go on and on, and many days I do. But one of the things I love God for is for sending his many masters and teachers like Jesus to the world. I love God for the many spirit helpers, like The Brotherhood of God and angels. I love God for the awakening that is still taking place in me and my family. I love God because He sat back and allowed me to make mistakes and to learn from them. I love God for teaching me to love as He does unconditionally. I wish I could say that I love this way all the time and love all people without condition. I do for the most part love unconditionally, but there are those times and those people who make it hard to comply with this way of loving.*

*I love God for the many insights and revelations that have come to me. I love God for realizations, such as, I am more than this body, more than my emotions, thoughts, beliefs, and intelligence. This is very freeing to know that I am more than what I see, and that there are greater purposes to life than what I can see, hear, feel, or smell. We all have greater hidden talents than we are aware of. Isn't it comforting to know this? It is to me. The very thought that there are greater talents within me has given me the inspiration to use the talents I know of. Once I let myself be inspired there have been more creative ideas than I can use.*

*So this Christmas I'm making a pledge to be grateful for Jesus, for his birth, and the beautiful story associated with it, to be grateful for his teachings and healings, and to be grateful for Jesus life. Now that I've learned to accept and value my life, I find it easier to love my neighbor as myself.*

*I hope you have a wonderful Christmas and/or Hanukkah. I hope you realize the great potential that is within you to accomplish, resolve issues, and to enjoy life. May the peace of God be a light to your search. May the example of Jesus' life be the road map for your inner life. And may you fully realize the great love God has for you.*

*Until next time, I remain your friend, —annie*

✧ ✧ ✧

**M**Y DEAR CHILDREN, I come to you in joy and in love. We are nearing the time you celebrate Jesus' birth. It is a joyous time, one that is a remembering of family and friends. I hope that in all your preparations you do not neglect your prayers and your meditations. It is important that you pray daily. It is more important that you take the time to meditate because this is the way to pay close attention to God. It is a good way to hear His silent voice.

Many of you will face times of trials and sorrow in the coming year. The last year of the Millennium is a time of letting go of the old, in one way or another. For the people who do not let go of the old joyfully and willingly, it can be traumatic. My children, listen and hear the still small voice within. Give yourself time to hear God as He directs you. Many of you will have a much easier time during the coming year. Regardless of how your life is going, I request that each of you spend time in prayer. I urge you to pray for each other. Pray for the children and young people. Pray for your loved ones, neighbors, and co-workers. Pray for humanity, because through each person's life and their experiences, humanity grows and progresses.

Pray for peace to come into the heart of each person on earth, that they may find the peace that passes all understanding, that they may find the love that God has for them. In this way, you are doing much to promote peace in the world. This is your mission, it is your gift to humanity.

When Jesus was born, the angels sang, "Peace on earth." They prayed for mankind to have good-will in their heart. This is still a good prayer today. Many of you have already made peace with your past, your present, and your future. You are already living in peace. As you continue to live with a sense of inner serenity and peace, you are doing much more than you realize to promote peace on earth. It takes a certain number of people to create that critical mass in order to have peace fairly explode throughout the consciousness of mankind. So each peaceful, loving prayer is important. Each peaceful, loving deed is important. Each peaceful, loving life is of the utmost importance.

My children, do all you can to live in peace. If your heart is still filled with anger and fear and all their depleting emotions, do all you can to rid yourself of these issues. Then do all you can to promote peace. You can promote peace through your prayers, most certainly. You can promote peace through your harmonious relationship with other people. You can take charge of your inner life and live a peaceful life. It is an innate ability within you to be able to live peacefully. You have simply forgotten how. You have allowed your pride and self-importance to take precedence. So do not shirk your responsibility to promote peace through your loving, compassionate actions. Each time you refuse to judge another person harshly, you promote peace. Each time you seek resolution to a problem, condition, or issue, you promote peace.

Carefully build a peaceful and harmonious relationship with yourself. Too many are much too harsh in their self-judgments. Be gentle with yourself, and you will be gentle and kind with others. Treat yourself as you wish for others to treat you. In this way you practice having harmonious relationships with yourself. Then, you will find this is your natural way to cope, to deal with others, and to demonstrate God's love. Peaceful living can be a reality on earth; it will take many, many people living peaceful, loving, non-judgmental lives in order it to be a reality for everyone.

When you are living in peace and in unconditional love, you will have a joy that is beyond what you know now. It is a joy that expresses itself in loving actions. It is a joy that is deeply satisfying and good. The joy of God brings pleasure to the small acts of life. Then it will be a joy to breathe, to see, to hear, to relate to others, to eat, and to do all the things the body needs in order to live on earth. Joy will be your natural make-up. Your humor will then be loving humor. Today people use derogatory remarks to insinuate humor. If it is hurtful to one person, it is not humor filled with joy. Joy is loving, it is understanding, and it is peaceful.

## PROMOTE PEACE

During this holiday season, when you remember the birth of the Christ child, set aside anything that does not promote peace, unconditional and true joy. This is a good time to christen yourself with a new name—you too can be called Immanuel. You can be a person of peace and understanding. Let the Spirit of Truth ring within you. Allow the Spirit of Truth to keep you motivated to peacefulness and to living in the Spirit of unconditional love. Christen yourself to promote a continuous, on-going communication with your Creator.

Allow the good-will which is felt during this time of the year to be carried into every day of your life. When you have an occasion to react in anger, remember your new name; you are here to bring peace into your heart, your life, and your world.

My dear little children, do not worry about when the next disaster will occur and where it will take place. Let all your energy, effort, and intent be towards the promotion of loving, peaceful living. Do all you can to be ready for any eventuality, then stay true to your new motivation, your new name. Do all things with an attitude of loving peacefulness. Respect all people and their beliefs, their choices in life, and in their way of life. Make no derogatory or harsh judgments in dealing with people. Seek to negotiate peace in any dispute. Settle all old angers and release all old fears. When you are with God, there is nothing to fear. Then, all will be in a Divine environment. Let all your intentions be good. Let all your workings and dealings be good. Work only for the good of the majority. But be good to yourself. Be good to your loved ones and give them the freedom God gives you. You are free to live your life in peace, love, and joy. You are free to choose goodness or wickedness. You are free to choose war or peace. Make the best choices. You can do this. I have confidence in you.

> Mary, Mother of Jesus.

# True Peace Is Alive

*2/99*

I HOPE YOU'RE HAVING A GREAT *1999. We started our New Year with our annual "Burning Ceremony." We keep a prayer basket in our home with all the requests people send either by mail, fax, or telephone call. On Sunday afternoons our meditation group meets. We place the prayer basket in our prayer circle. During the week I pray for all the people whose names are in the basket, and on Sunday the group prays.*

*The last week of the year, or at times the first Sunday of the year, we burn all the prayer requests as a symbol of our willingness to surrender. In order to be fair and allow those who write after Halloween to have a full year, I save those requests and put them into the basket after the burning. Mother Mary and the Brotherhood have taught us about the need to release and surrender our requests in order to have them answered. I keep getting this message, "Let the request go." Once you are satisfied that your prayer states exactly what you are thinking, feeling, and wanting, then it's time to surrender. I've found it best to tell God all about the subject, or person, I'm praying for or about. I tell God the obvious, what I'm anticipating, and what I'm meaning by the words I'm using. Then when I'm satisfied that I've not left anything out, I surrender.*

*But back to the prayer basket. Since the prayer requests in the basket are not my prayers, it seemed a little presumptuous to try to decide what is wanted or needed by the people. So I simply write out your name and place it in the prayer basket, or I put your letter or envelope in. My feeling is that God is listening as you pray. I'm supporting your prayer. Mother Mary said that prayer is accumulative and for that reason I believe that all supporting prayers help. Since I don't always hear back from people if their prayer is answered or not, there had to be a cut-off time. A time to surrender. I chose the end of the calendar year.*

*So on the Sunday after Christmas, or the Sunday after New Years, we hold a burning ceremony. We meet as usual and after the meditation we burn all the prayer requests in the prayer basket. Also we burn old calendars or a list of the things we do not want to carry into the New Year. For instance, you can list any old reoccurring behavior, or thought patterns like procrastination, obsessing, self-sabotage, or simply not sticking to a diet. We list everything that we can think of. Then we burn it all in our wood stove. You can use a stainless steel bowl, wok, or the kitchen sink. It's not what you burn your prayer request and list in, it's the intention, thought, and motivation behind the burning. By the way, please be careful when burning your prayers.*

*Mother Mary urged us to make a list of goals for the year. We were taught to consider all the areas of our life; family, career, spiritual, health, self-improvement, recreation, educational, and such. Goals, as I define it, are the things, situations, attitudes, and desires I want in my life now. A year ago Byron and I were talking about what we would like to see happen in our business, B&A Products. I set a sales goal, realizing that at best it was a very high hope. It just didn't seem feasible at the time. Nothing else was said about the goal during the year, nor did I think about it again. At the end of the year we realized that we had surpassed it.*

*What this demonstrated to me is the power of surrender. I set that goal, praying in a very informal way that we would achieve it. Then feeling it was a very, very high hope, I let it go. I remember what I used to tell my sons, "Wish upon a star, you just might get the moon." If only it were just as easy to let go of other prayer requests. I find it easier to surrender the things I hope for than the things I truly want. So I just keep on praying, knowing that when the time is right, I may get it, or something better.*

*In all this rambling, what I'm trying to say is, if you sent in a prayer request last year and still want us to continue to pray with you, let us know. We will be happy to support your prayers, with the understanding that you will get the answer, or the request will be fulfilled in a way that is for your highest good.*

*Haven't you found that when you look back, that many of your prayers have been answered better than you had first imagined? Or have you noticed that sometimes your prayers start out looking like a disaster? In the new messages coming through now, Mother Mary says that sometimes God has to get us ready to receive the request. Many times Mother Mary says we have to heal or let go of old habits, thought patterns, or simply some of our "stuff" in order to receive what we've prayed for.*

*Anyway, the whole idea behind this letter is to let you know that if we were supporting you in prayer last year and you feel you still need our support, or if you would like us to support your prayers, just write and tell us. If it makes you feel better to get things off your chest by writing about it, that's ok. If you don't want to tell us what you are praying for, that's ok. No one, ever sees your written request except me. We don't take the prayer requests out of the basket once they are placed there. I do my best to keep it all confidential.*

*We thank you for your continued support and your prayers. This is a two-way street. I support you just as you support us. Our love goes out to you. Until next time. —annie*

◇ ◇ ◇

M Y DEAR CHILDREN, it is with great pleasure that I come to you in joy and with a deep abiding peace. It is the peace that passes all understanding. This is the peace that is awaiting you. In this peace are all the components of God's, love . . . non-judgmental, non-restricting, and non-limiting.

There is joy . . . a happiness that is comforting, deep, and abiding. There is understanding . . . that gives you solace, consolation to the soul, and a satisfaction to the spirit. There is power . . . the power to go beyond pride and willfulness. There is strength . . . the courage to change the things in your life that need changing. There is life . . . a vibrancy that gives a lift to the spirit. There is serenity . . . the stillness of the soul and the serenity that accepts without thought that which cannot be changed. There is gratitude . . . a deep recognition of one's blessings.

Peace is more than the mere cessation of antipathy. True peace is alive, just as love is alive. Many of you pray for peace but do not have peaceful hearts. Realize that what you know about peace is very limited. There is nothing limiting about peace, in contrast everything about war is limiting and destructive. So consider that there are many small wars taking place everyday in the work place, in homes and sadly in churches. These small wars are inhibiting peace. Are you inhibiting peace? Do you carry on with a feud that perhaps was not of your making? Do you have a resentful, contentious soul? Do you still judge yourself and others harshly? Do you covet what others have in their hearts, soul, or life? All these things harbingers of bigger issues, which in turn, bring about war.

My dear children, put away the hurt, pride, and injured feelings. Let nothing stand in the way of living your life in peace. True peace is lived in an atmosphere of unconditional love. The peace that passes all understanding comes from a loving, accepting, and forgiving heart. You do more good for mankind and Earth when you forgive one small injury. When you struggle to forgive the larger damage done by abuse and addiction, you do greater good for mankind. Peace has a difficult time remaining in a raging, angry life. Peace comes to the world from inside of you. How can you talk about love, and peace, yet live with resentment toward family members? How many of you promote peace from a secretive and angry heart?

Let your heart heal from all injuries from all long held injury. Make every effort to settle old disputes, to be at peace with your family and neighbors. When you do your best to live in peace, then the Spirit of Truth and Peace will assist you. There are many who pray for peace, it is now time to live your prayer. It is time to live in peace . . . total, undemanding, and loving peace.

Strive to bring all the components of peace into your life. Become peaceful by setting aside your harsh judgments. Perform the settling of old disputes in joy. You may shed tears; they will be good, cleansing tears. It is better for you to shed your tears, than to allow them to be buried deep within your heart. It is better to settle disputes immediately, to forgive instantly, than to live in an angry, warring way. You can begin to allow the joy of peace to fill your life.

To allow the joy of peace to live in your heart is a decision. You can choose to live the rest of your days on Earth in joyful peace, or you can not make a decision and allow your life to drift along. When you fail to make the choice, then you are at the mercy of circumstances. You drift along through life, like driftwood, neither making any choices or having any dominion over your life. You allow the choices of others, the situations and circumstances of others to rule over you. It is time, my children, to take command of your life. It is time to choose peace, instead of contention. It is time to decide and take responsibility for changing the way mankind thinks, feels, and reacts.

You want peace on earth? Then live that desire every day of your life. You want to be happy? Allow the joy that is a part of peace, to dictate your reactions to life's circumstances. You want to help others? Then allow peace to come to this world, through your heart, decisions, and life. Peace comes to earth through you. The peace that is filled with joy, love, understanding, power, and strength to fill you with determination to live each day in peace.

Let God's understanding begin to be the way you relate to others. Do all you can to understand, and where you cannot understand the other person, be accepting. When you accept people for themselves, instead of for what they can do, give, or bring to you, then you are loving unconditionally. Let the joy of peace fill you with strength. Being peaceful must come from your inner self. If you concentrate on the outer part of you, then you are not making the deep changes that can turn lives from war to peace. Being peaceful is more than looking serene, it is more than hiding from difficult issues. Being peaceful means you are strong enough to love without limit, without thought of changing the other person. Being peaceful means that you have the power to make a decision and to see that decision manifested in your life. Being peaceful means you appreciate life and strive to make your life a living example of God's love, peace, and truth.

My children, heed these words. Take them into your heart of hearts. Become peaceful now. Allow yourself the pleasure of living in joyful peace, to recognize the understanding that comes with peace, and the strength that is a part of peace. You can live your life in joyful peace. Begin by concentrating on cleansing your heart and mind of all that is not peaceful. Make peace with your past, present, and future. This means that you no longer are hurtful, angry, fearful of any event or situation from the past which now causes you to be out of peace. It also means that you concentrate on staying peaceful. To do so, you will forgive immediately, love unconditionally, and have the courage and strength to make the changes necessary to live in peace. You can do this, my children. You go within to find the spark or flame of peace that lies within your heart of hearts.

I keep you in my prayers and in my heart. I love you as God does.

Mary, Mother of Jesus.

# 45

## Pray for Peace

4/99

ISN'T SPRING WONDERFUL? *It wasn't until I saw the first daffodils and hyacinths that I realized I've been in a blue funk for several weeks. We have had quite a few changes in our home and business. Our son, James and his fiancee, Amy, have come to live and work with us. I'm very grateful they could come into the business to help out since it has gotten so busy. I wish I could adapt and adjust with grace.*

*I've had some internal adjustment to make: attitude, awareness, thinking before speaking. My rabble-rouser nature is alive and well. I really love having them here. They add energy, vitality, fun, and enjoyment to our daily lives. I'm learning to be a mother without mothering, something parents get a chance to learn sooner or later. I'm also learning to keep my opinions to myself and to allow them to be.*

*As you already know, I've had to learn to set boundaries and speak up when I need something. I'm practicing once again. You'd think I'd finally get it. Throughout my lifetime I've engaged in what my therapist calls passive-aggressive behavior. Many women of my generation learned to react this way; we learned from experts, our mothers and grandmothers. What I've come to realize is that my mother was born at the end of the Victorian age, when nice ladies didn't say bad things, they just showed through their behavior that* they were displeased. If I don't watch myself, I will revert to these behaviors, without thinking. I get quiet or snipe, mostly at my husband and son. I have all kinds of small snotty remarks to make instead of speaking in a calm, loving voice. What I'm relearning is to speak from my truth, to clearly and concisely say what I need to say in a loving voice. I'm proud to say I don't place blame any longer.

For a few days my reaction to the changes were unreasonable and certainly unloving. It bothered me and made me feel bad and not peaceful. So I've been praying for and about me. In meditation I heard, "You advocate and stress family. Now it's time to practice new ways of living with your family." The new ways I feel are to change my passive-aggressive behavior to loving, compassionate behavior. I hope I've not acted this way with Amy, but I have with Byron and James. Isn't that the way it goes—we are so comfortable with our family that we expect them to understand what we are feeling without speaking words. It sounds like I've been a tee-total witch, but the truth is I used to be a lot worse. Nowadays, I catch myself being out of peace.

Then there is this blue funk that has been like a cloud. I don't know how much of this funk has been due to the rapid changes taking place and how much is due to the fibromyalgia acting up. It really doesn't matter. I'd gotten out of my peaceful inner state and have been acting from anger instead of love. So it's back to a basic lesson in peace. I get to practice, and do what it takes to get back into my peaceful state of mind.

I don't like being out of peace, it feels bad, not comfortable, and certainly makes me feel like a bad person. These are the feelings that send up a red flag for me. They say, "Alert, alert! You're not peaceful, what's happened?" So I begin to look within and see what is going on. I've been blessed with many very good friends, both in Dallas and here in Oklahoma. It helps to speak to one or two of them about what I'm feeling. One of the things that happens to me is that I get confused and can't see what is really bothering me. Talking to a good friend helps me cut through to the real issues. When I know the real issue, then I can make decisions, change my attitude, and find ways to address the issues. Most times a change in *attitude helps me tremendously. Many times what I thought was bothering me goes away with a change of attitude. I say to myself, "You are not being peaceful or loving right now. I choose and make a conscious decision to be peaceful and loving in handling this situation." I use this affirmation until it is done.*

*Wasn't it Lincoln who said, "People are about as happy as they decide to be," or something like that? I remember that I always have a choice. Daily I can choose to be angry and hateful, or I can choose to be peaceful and loving, I can choose to be happy and see the good in my life. Or, if I fail to choose, I revert to my old ways and see the bad in everything. Living my life in peace is a conscious choice. It's an undertaking that requires me to be alert and aware. I must be honest and concentrate on how I'm doing in my inner life and not what family members are doing. I'm responsible for taking care of me. This frees my family to handle their problems and stresses in their own way.*

*So now that spring is here and things are just beginning to flower, I feel great. It really is like resurrecting. I've left my old funky, warring self behind and feel that I've been lifted up into a new awareness of my peaceful nature. I'm truly blessed with a loving family.*

*Mother Mary urges us to live peaceful lives. What I've found is that I must make a concerted effort to return to peace when I find myself feeling bad and warlike. Most often who I fight is myself. My stuff can raise its ugly head from time to time. Usually it happens when I've gone brain dead and am not conscious of my reactions. We are not allowed to fake this. In the seventies I heard people say, "Just fake it." That will not work now. Now is the time of truth. In order to bring peace into the world, each of us needs to watch our reactions, actions, thoughts, and relationships to be sure we are acting from a peaceful, loving nature. It requires that we be totally honest with ourselves and that we return to an inner peaceful state of mind quickly when we get out of it. Anyway that's what is going on with me. I really appreciate your friendship and support. My best to you and I pray that you are having wonderful lives. Until next time, I remain your friend. —annie*

## PRAY FOR PEACE

✧ ✧ ✧

My Dear Children, I come today with a petition and a request that you increase your time of prayer and meditation and that you pray for the war-torn areas. Many are suffering needlessly because of politics. This is true of many areas in the world. You are aware of one area which is along the Adriatic Sea. You know that my apparitions in Yugoslavia have been going on for years. I love this area and pray that the people will see the similarities in their lives and not the differences. There are many who seek their own benefit to the exclusion of others. Yet within this area are many who are faithful and true to God. Pray for everyone no matter which faction they belong to. Do not pray for one side to win and the other side to lose. Pray that people will seek to live in peace. Pray for negotiations to begin that will bring all parties together for the purpose of peace.

Pray for the people on the African continent, as they too face many challenges. There is much suffering in many nations. I talk about the suffering of the spirit, and not only of the body. People suffer when they are enslaved in any way. People's spirit can flourish under the most dire conditions, but you who have plenty, who have the time and the energy to help others, are urged to help through your prayer.

Many times people believe that if they pray they are not doing enough. Yet it is prayer that does the most good and causes the greatest changes in the consciousness of mankind. When you pray, you are sending your love, your concern, your hope, your energy, your thoughts, and your spirit. Yet you think this is very little. When people pray in mass for someone or something, there is wholeness that infuses the person or situation. Pray with fervor, putting your spirit and energy into your prayers. This is how to help the most.

While you are praying for these war-torn areas, do not indulge in talking about how bad it is, or how terrible the situation is. Maintain your faith in the Goodness of God. Seek instead to see the concern and the love that people have for their fellow human, no matter their circumstances. Set aside your judgments, let your mind be filled with hope for a good outcome. In this way you open yourself, your life, and allow your prayers to be infused with more power. Your country is one which is caught up in trying to right a wrong. Stay away from thinking that this country is right and the other country is wrong. The countryside and the people are not to blame. It is politics and the will of a few people who are causing the suffering of many.

You help when you give yourself up to prayer. You help more than you can understand. You are a part of mankind. It is your responsibility and duty to pray for your fellow humans. Many people would rather give something: money, food, clothes, something tangible. This is good and needed in many cases. But you give more through prayer than mere goods; you give from your spirit. It is the spirit that remains alive throughout time. It is the spirit that can give the gifts of life, of goodness, of wholeness, and of love. To pray, then, is the greatest gift you can give another.

My little children, I ask you to give from your spirit and from your truth, for then you are giving from your heart of hearts. You can avert many catastrophes through prayer. You can change the course of mankind with your prayers. Together you can change the consciousness when you use the gifts of the spirit, such as when you love unconditionally. This is why I ask you not to make judgments, not to speak of the horror of the situation. Instead I ask you to love all people, even those who are causing the war, and those who are participating in the war.

Give your thoughts, your intentions, your motivations to living in peace. Do this not only for yourself and your loved ones, but for humanity. Think in peaceful terms, in your inner life and in your dealings with others. Where there is controversy or ill feelings in your family or among friends, do all you can to bring about peaceful solutions. Where there is strife of any kind, seek to negotiate peaceful endings. In order for there to be peace in the world, its people must begin to live daily with a deep inner peace. This is the only way for peace to come to the world.

As you live your life in peace, ending all feuds, settling all issues, forgiving all that keeps you from peace, you are increasing the consciousness of mankind towards goodness, towards peace. As you realize that all people are loved by God, the Father, you help to turn the race consciousness towards peace. You have the capability to do much good for the world, simply by living your life in peace. You have the ability to pray with your whole spirit, soul, and heart. This is how to bring peace into the world. There is much each of you can do to instill peace into the consciousness of mankind. Never feel powerless, for through your prayers, and especially as you unite in prayer, you can bring peace into the world.

So many of you want to do great things for mankind. You want to go to other countries or other cities to teach, to perform musically, to preach, when what is needed is for each person to live their life with a deep inner peace and serenity. Settling old unresolved angers, facing and overcoming your fears, forgiving those who have hurt you in any way, is the best way to do great things. Spending time in quiet prayer is the highest and the best gift you can offer. There is no need to run throughout the countryside trying to bring about peace. If you seek to achieve peace through mechanical means, through the doing, preforming, or giving without having a peaceful heart, you waste your time and energy. You must live what you seek to give to others.

Be grateful for the peace you have already achieved. Let your heart be filled with gratitude for the simple things in life—for the continuity of life, for the changing season, for the laughter and joy that is a part of your life. Be grateful for the love that God has for you. Be grateful for the talents you have, for the life you are living. Be grateful for all things, and with a grateful heart you will see ways to achieve a peaceful inner life and the deep serenity that comes through prayer.

There is much you can do in the quietness of your mind, in the meditations of your heart. I have confidence in you. I would not request this of you if it were not possible for you to achieve it. You are more capable than you realize. I am loving each of you greatly.

Mary, Mother of Jesus.

# 46

## Conclave for Peace

6/99

WELL, JUST WHEN I THINK I'VE GOT IT, *I'm given even bigger, tougher lessons. Maybe it's the way I'm able to learn, or maybe it's just the way it is. Hopefully, one day in the near future I will be able to share these very painful and tough lessons with you. For now, I request your prayers for me and my family. Before you let your imagination go wild, let me assure you that Byron and I are strongly united in a very loving marriage.*

*A few days ago I received a delightful e-mail that had the subject listed as, "Annie, you are human after all." I'm aware I'm having a human experience. That has never been a problem for me. What I remind myself of is that I am spirit having this human experience and that there is more to me than this one lifetime. For a time, I've thought of my life as being my spirit life, the one I'm living eternally now. In talks, I've said I'm probably nine billion and forty years old now and will live for who knows how long. I don't believe I've had all these different, chopped up lives. I believe what Mother Mary said in Her first messages is true . . . we live eternally. We are living it now, not at some later date, or after death.*

*What I'm living now is only one of many life experiences I've had on earth. It's a very human experience, one that has been filled with very happy and good experiences and some very painful, angry, and fearful experiences . . . but all of it has been very human. One of the things that can happen to people who are blessed with receiving messages from Mother Mary or other Divine messages is that we can begin to identify with the messages and the Being giving the messages. Thank God this hasn't been a problem for me. In fact, I still question how this could've happened to me. It's not false humility or a low self-esteem that causes me to question. It's more that I'm aware of my human frailties and human reactions.*

*Then one wouldn't necessarily have to be receiving any Divine messages to become a spiritual elitist. I've known people in organized religions who are religious elitists. You know them because they think their way is the only way to God, and since they have already completed the required things in order to be highly religious, they are in and you are out. Then we have the people who believe that to be spiritual you must read the right books, perform the "right" rituals or ceremonies, or that you must teach meditation or "do something." They most assuredly are very spiritual because, after all, they are doing it.*

*Once Mother Mary told me that giving a lecture, workshop, or leading a meditation group is not my spiritual work. She said that is my service. My spiritual work involves clearing away the unresolved angers, overcoming my fears, settling old family issues. My spiritual work is when I allow the Spirit of God to work in me, to heal. It's when I face the truth about myself, my life, and how I've lived it.*

*I feel that separating ourselves into the ins and the outs is not being spiritual. I think that anything that separates us from our fellow humans is detrimental to our own spirit and the spirit of humanity.*

*God/Spirit always comes through for me. Just when I think, "Thank God, I think I've finally got it," I get other lesson, usually having to do with my family of origin and/or my present family unit of husband and children. There is nothing like having a family out of peace, out of sync, to bring you up short. When I'm relating to my family, I often have a lot of doubts about how I'm handling things. I can fall into my past behavior of co-dependency, or more to the point, fight against falling back into that behavior. A good friend of mine reminded me that when I fall in with co-dependent people, I*

## CONCLAVE FOR PEACE

*feel yucky, sticky, and bad. Now that's my signal that things are not right, no matter how good they appear on the outside. Sometimes I'm a little slow to realize what I'm feeling.*

*It seems as soon as Mother Mary requests something of people, I get the privilege of learning it firsthand. I left off being a drama queen a long time ago. Now when something dramatic happens, I know it's Spirit's way of getting my attention fast. For me drama is synonymous with loud. So when I first heard the words, "Hold a Conclave for Peace," I was already in a situation in which there was little peace. I was working hard to stay in serenity, while living in a very unsettling situation.*

*One day when I was facing some unpeaceful "stuff," I received a call from a friend in Dallas. He didn't know anything about the situation I was in. In our chat he was telling me about Father Leo Booth, an Episcopalian priest in California who works in the 12 step/recovery field, and has written several books. This priest has a favorite saying that I have now adopted for myself. The saying is, "Screw nice, be real." I laughed and commented that I often get into more trouble when I try to be nice. Haven't you had those situations where someone takes advantage of you and you tell yourself, it really doesn't matter and that you must be nice? That's one of the things that happened to me. So now I am just trying like heck to be real. If I don't like something, I've promised myself to speak up. Speaking up is another lesson I still practice.*

*Anyway, right now I'm in the middle of learning once again how to be real, which to me is also being human. We came into this life to live a very real, human experience. There's a lot to say for being human. It brings many good, humorous experiences, and many heart-wrenching experiences. All in all, it's been a good life, and I expect it to continue to be good, even through the tough times.*

*Well, until next time, I remain your friend, —annie*

⋄ ⋄ ⋄

My Dear Children, I come to you once again in love and with peace. As more and more people are praying for peace, you are finding that turmoil is becoming evident in dramatic ways. Do not for one minute think that your prayers are failing, or that there is something wrong. In order to have peace there is much to forgive and heal. We need more prayers for peace and less judgment.

In your personal lives you may experience the turmoil that is seen in the events of the world. That which needs to be forgiven rises from the depths of you, in order that it may be seen in truth. It is calling attention to problems, situations, and people you need to release in forgiveness. Continue to pray for peace because it is working. Pray that all events, both personal and global are seen in truth. It is not wise to hide from the truth. For when you know the truth of any given situation, you will know what to do and how to do it.

In global events, you forgive for yourself and for humanity. Whereever there is a tragedy which involves several people, begin immediately to forgive. Not that you were harmed, but that mankind was harmed. You, as a part of mankind and humanity, can begin the forgiveness process. Where there is war, refuse to take sides; instead pray for all parties involved as you pray for a peaceful solution. It is important that you pray for all factions involved in the situation.

You can do much to advance the progress of mankind. You can pray for humanity to know the truth—the truth of any given situation and the truth about all global affairs. Many of your fellow humans are suffering and their suffering is not revealed. There are many places where people are abused, tormented, and killed. Just as there are many homes where abuse is happening now. In many families brother is pitted against brother, addictions are harming the family. There are many circumstances in which people take advantage of each other, and this causes much pain.

There are many who need to be supported with your prayers. You need the support of your fellow human beings' prayers. This is my first call to you. Pray as you never have before. Pray for yourself and your loved ones. Pray for those who oppose you and for people around you who behave in unloving ways. Pray for the world without judging the events of the world. Pray for tomorrow, for the future. Pray for family circumstances, whether they are happy or sad, loving or fearful, uplifting or despairing, just or unjust.

Now my children, I call you to a "Conclave for Peace," to gather together to pray for peace, to hold the image of peaceful families, peaceful cities, and peaceful settlements. Use the date, August 15th, to gather for this purpose. I call you to come together for a day of peace. Talk about personal issues which are keeping you from living in peace with each other, then pray for these issues. Sing songs of peace. Music allows you to voice in a harmonious way your desire for peace. Read poems of peace, state thoughts for peace. Talk about how you can begin to live in peace if you are not already. Talk about how you are already resolving, settling, and healing situations and circumstances in your life for peace.

I will be present on that day in many places. Gather in churches, gather in homes, and gather in beautiful places of nature, by lakes, streams, and oceans, in meadows, mountain tops and deserts. Let yourself become peaceful, for one day. When as large a group as two or three gather in my Son's name, we are all present. When you gather together for conclaves for peace, you do much to further peaceful states of being in individual people, families, cities, and in countries.

Always begin within yourself. It is time to be peaceful, as peaceful as you can be. Live in peace and turn away from the people, circumstances, and conditions that keep you from living in peace. It is time to love all people and to love without becoming enmeshed in their lives. It is time to free yourself and others to find peace in their own way, and in their own time.

I call you to choose peace. But understand, it is not always as you think. Many people have preconceived ideas of peace. Peace, just like love, must be unconditional. Peace comes to people in many different ways. Remember my children, that in order to live peaceful lives, first settle and resolve old issues which have been keeping you from a peaceful life. So many of you will feel the sting of despair in the beginning. That is because you must let go of hurt feelings, hurt pride, and angry, unresolved matters. You may find many things rising from the ashes of the past to be forgiven and released.

Do not let yourself be fooled, this too is the road to peace. So live in peace each day to the best of your ability. Let each day begin with prayer and end with prayer. Let each day stand alone without judgment and without doubt. When a family member or fellow human is living in difficult circumstances, let this be your call to pray for them instead of talking about them. Talk is helpful when it is used to clear away the angers, fears, resentment and envies from your life. You do not help a person by passing along gossip that is detrimental.

Use your words to heal, to speak your truth, to uplift, and to bless. The first person to heal is you; the only situations to heal are those which involve you personally. The rest is healed through prayer. Speak of what is true of you; do not allow another person to speak for you. Instead take the responsibility for speaking your truth when and where it is needed. Many times people do not want to speak about what they are truly feeling or what they are truthfully seeking. Fear enters and closes your mouths or alters your words. The time to speak your truth is when you are feeling out-of-sorts. Then is the time to look within to see what you are truly feeling, what is truthfully bothering you. Do not sugarcoat the truth. Please speak your truth with tact and kindness. If that is not possible, then speak your truth as you can.

Unite with me to pray for peace. I am pleased with your faithfulness. Many have already made the commitment to live in peace. Many of you have been working through the issues of life on earth. You can do much to bring peace into the world through your own life. Remember always my love is with you.

Mary, Mother of Jesus.

# Increase Your Faith

8/99

*T*IME SEEMS TO HAVE DONE ANOTHER DOUBLING. *Isn't this year speeding by, or is it my imagination? During the first half of this year, I was ery busy. Even though my life was at a fast pace, the lessons continued.*

*I've learned something else about forgiveness. Forgiveness and resolution are not the same thing. We have a rift in our family. It has been very heartbreaking. The other person and myself agree that we love each other—that hasn't changed. We, who have never had a rift in our immediate family, are now dealing with a problem that many families face. I began the forgiveness process immediately, even when I didn't feel very forgiving. Because of the anger and hurt feelings this situation brought up for me, I threw dozens and dozens of eggs at a tree, to release the emotion. Now, after several months of working on it, I am at peace most of the time. I still have periods where I grieve for our family.*

*Soon after Mother Mary's visits began, She required me to "Live her message." In the beginning I didn't know what that meant. I decided that what She asked me to do, was to pray, forgive, and love, etc. She also said I was to live this message in my own way. Now it seems that my family is giving me a great opportunity to go a step further in living the message. It's by returning to the* serenity that I had lost in this troubling, heart-wrenching, and difficult situation.

This month I'm hosting a "Conclave for Peace" in our home. I was wondering how I could host anything related to peace without resolving this issue. It's a little embarrassing to be focused on peace and have this kind of thing arise in my life. Then I remembered the first time Mother Mary asked to teach "Peace" in my own town, at that time Dallas. Three days before the workshop on peace, we were served with the notice that our neighborhood association had filed a lawsuit against us. Byron had put up a small, slender, ham radio antenna, which they objected to. The day before the workshop, I cried out to Mother Mary that I didn't feel very peaceful when my neighbors were at war with us. I was told to be honest with the people, and I was. It seems that mandate still stands, so hence the honesty in spite of the embarrassment.

So often people think that because of my visitations from the Blessed Mother, I lead a perfect life. But what has happened is that I've kept on living my life without too much Divine intervention. Certainly not a utopian life, but one that is constantly improving as I keep "Living the message."

I'm still learning that to love unconditionally does not mean I become a doormat. In fact, now that I love myself unconditionally, I'm better able to take care of myself. Although, as I found out, I can regress to my bad habits, like not speaking up for myself at the right time and with calmness, thinking that by ignoring something that doesn't feel right the problem will go away, and by trying to be nice, instead of real. Thankfully, I've learned to set boundaries very well. The love that allows me to be strong is unconditional love. I can be strong and understand that the other person in a dispute is just as strong in their spirit.

Then came the great revelation that forgiveness and resolution are not the same. The concept of forgiving was easy, because I love my family unconditionally. On one hand it was easy to begin to forgive, and on the other it was difficult because of the anger and anguish. Going past the hurt and all the old issues, this incident hooked into was a stumbling block. So I went back to the first step, which is learning to love myself, and in loving myself, I took care of myself by stopping the situation. I must admit that, had I done this sooner, I would have been gentler and quieter in speaking my truth. But I did speak my truth, finally.

Forgiveness was easier once I had released most of the anger by throwing eggs at my egg tree. I'm still working on the process. Most of all I'm forgiving myself for the way I handled it. If I had to do it over again, the only thing I would change is the way I spoke my truth. Have you ever played Monday morning quarterback with yourself? Have you not found that the best responses often come afterwards. Do you go over confrontations and wish you had said it differently? I've found this doesn't bring you peace, it keeps you obsessing on the event. I must admit that I've had a difficult time letting it go. And I believe with my whole heart that I must let it go in order for God to work through us to bring about a healing.

The situation is not resolved, but I'm at peace knowing that I'm well into the process of forgiveness, that I can be at peace, even though it is not settled. Both parties must come together in order for there to be resolution. But we don't need anyone else to have a peaceful heart. Once again I'm reminded that I can't change anyone except myself, that all I have to work with is me, and the only one I have to change is me.

One of Mother Mary's prayer requests is for the family, because She says too many families are at war. I think this is what She is talking about. It's not the shoot-um-up wars but the disputes that linger, the failure to respect each other and their property, and it's trying to fix each other. We can be at peace even in the midst of disputes. It's all about bringing peace into the world, one day at a time, one incident at a time, one life at a time, and one family at a time.

Until next time, join me in really, really praying for peace to come to each of us today. We can make a difference in our world, when we pray for peace. —annie

## INCREASE YOUR FAITH

My Dear Children, I come to you in love and peace. My greatest hope is that you fully understand how much you are loved. And that you understand what this means to you as you go through life. As you come to understand the all-encompassing love that is within you, around you, and permeated in you, your faith will grow. You will be able to trust God implicitly.

Your complete trust in God's love will increase your faith tremendously. You will have the faith that can and will move mountains. Jesus had this kind of faith. Never once did he doubt that God would cease to love him. His faith was based on the full knowledge of the extent and magnitude of God's love. Do you have this kind of faith? Faith of this kind goes all the way to your soul and spirit.

To have total trust and complete faith in God is a good way to allow peace to flourish in your heart, your life, and your surroundings. Do all you can to increase your concept of God's love. Stop the murmuring and discordant resentments. Leave the grievances and judgments of others alone. You cannot fully understand God's love while you are holding on to bitterness, anger, hatred, fears, envy, or any of these kinds of emotions. It is past the time to put these things aside. Only you can do this. God will help you if you call upon Him. But remember my little children, God will not work for you, He only works through you.

All of God's gifts are made without any strings or contingencies attached. When God gave the gift of freedom of choice, it was made in this way. God will not supersede your will unless it is for the greater good of humanity. All your choices are honored, respected, and adhered to. For this reason it is important that you make your individual choices about your life. It is still up to you to act in order for God to work through you. The action which is the best is an action of the spirit. It is to maintain faith, to trust that God is helping you in all things.

Many times people feel hopeless as they pray. This is not having faith; it is not trusting God. With God all things are possible. He could remake this world in the twinkling of an eye. He could recreate the universe in the time it takes you to take a breath. God is giving you the opportunity to experience life through your choices. You have so many choices and so many opportunities to make your life one of peace, love, and joy. You can find all that you need to live your life, within yourself. It is up to you to learn to use your faith in such a way that it grows and increases.

Jesus told you many years ago that it takes very little faith to do wondrous things. He compared the amount of faith needed to a mustard seed. That is a very small amount. You can increase your faith by using it. Faith grows as you use it.

How do you use faith? For many of you it is through the repetition of affirmations of faith. The words you use help you implant the concept in your mind and heart, so that you understand. Affirmations of faith also remind you of what you believe. Belief is very important to your life. Belief is what you base your life on. It is how you live your life and conduct your life. So do not belittle the need to increase your faith. Instead recognize its importance in your life.

Take a close look at what you believe. Are you living up to your belief, or are you living down from your belief? It will be easier to increase your faith if you are living up to your belief. So many of you do not give any thought to your beliefs, and if asked, would respond in vague, popular, and general terms. This is why I'm asking you to scrutinize your beliefs, to take a quiet moment to answer the above question. It will help you tremendously to find out if your beliefs correspond to how you are living today.

Pray about your faith. Ask God to help you increase your faith. For out of your belief, out of your faith, your life will be made so much better. The lack of faith causes you to stay in unpleasant circumstances. God will give to you according to your faith. If you really, really believe, deep down in your heart of hearts that what you ask for is right for you, is possible, and will improve your life, then it will be given unto you.

But you ask about the things you have prayed for believing they were right, possible, and would improve your life, yet you have not received them. Many things can cause you to lose faith, but this question seems to be the one that causes you the most difficulty. Sometimes it is not a lack of faith, or that you did not pray correctly. It could well be that you are obstinate about how this is to be provided. Preconceived notions, and wanting something to come the way you want it to come, can deter the answer to your prayer.

When you pray, my children, have the faith that the answer to your prayer will come to you the way God wants to send it. So many times what you pray for is not the whole of what you need. So God sees what is best for you and all the people involved in the prayer, and He answers in a way that is best for everyone concerned. Review your unanswered prayers; you may have already received the answer in a much better way.

God will not interfere in your choices. He will not interfere in anyone's choices. God gives the best He can according to your faith, what is best for the situation, and what is best for your whole life. Rest assured that, when you leave something in God's hands, the situation will work out in a way that everyone concerned is improved, according to their belief.

Think on this—it is so much easier to trust a loving God than it is to trust an angry God. The Truth is . . . that God is love. It is out of His great love that He answers your prayers. He forgives you all things. His love is Divine and unconditional. You can rely on this with your whole life.

Have faith that when you pray for people to open their hearts and minds to peace, it will be done. Place your focus in life on peace, on love, and on wisdom. Where you focus your life is how you will live, how your life will unfold, and it will unfold according to your faith. Never fear, for God is always as near as your heartbeat. He hears you when you call out to Him. Have faith in this.

I am loving you as you go through your life. Thank you for listening.

Mary, Mother of Jesus.

# 48

## *Prayer Brings Change*

10/99

ONCE AGAIN WE HAD THE HONOR *of hosting an open house, and it's astounding the pleasure that comes from seeing our friends and supporters once again. We had the added benefit of meeting new friends. I thank all of you who took the time and made the effort to come early and made a special weekend even more memorable. I really appreciate all the help you were.*

Mother Mary once again made Her presence known. Many, including myself, had the privilege of seeing her. It's always amazing how many wonderful ways She has shown Herself to me. This year I again saw the standing Madonna figure in deep blue with pink all around it, which is how I usually see Her. The Madonna has shadows that indicate eyes, nose, and mouth. Later as the sun was setting, I saw the Blessed Mother in an oval, like She was inside a cameo pin, but facing more toward the front instead of a profile. This time Jesus was present. In my mind's eye I saw Jesus as a child with Joseph standing to the right of the cameo. All the time we were watching the sun spin, change colors, and I could see the Madonna figure, I was experiencing auditory messages. Jesus said he came as a child to remind me that I had to keep the innocence of a child. I took this to mean that I needed to keep innocent in order to truly experience peace and to never doubt that I am at peace, no matter what is happening in my life.

*During the time I was seeing Mary, I was receiving messages. I share those messages that are placed in my heart to share. Mary asked us to observe the 15th of every month as a day of prayer for peace. She again reminded me that we have to begin to live peaceful lives. I forgot one message, and maybe it's for you, if you too joined us that day to pray for world peace. Mother Mary said we would each receive an individual revelation. She urged us not to guess how or what these revelations would be. Mother Mary said they would come to us as either an idea, an insight, advice, or a suggestion. We will recognize it as a revelation.*

*There was a man who dropped in just as we were putting away the lunch leftovers. He was on the highway going from California to Georgia. He said he had no intention of coming here and he didn't know why he was here. His wife had wanted to come, but not him. He looked like he felt out of place, yet he stayed. Just as we were leaving Lake Tenkiller, after the apparition, he said to me, "I got my message. I know why I was supposed to be here." Then I received a call from a friend who has attended these apparitions in the past. She had recently had lung surgery and was unable to attend this year. She said, "I prayed and watched the sunset. I saw pink in the sky and felt deep down in my gut that I would be healed. It was just a deep knowingness." So without me telling anyone, people were already receiving their revelations.*

*After the sun set and was gone from the horizon, the group formed a large circle and we ended singing "Amazing Grace" and what I call "the peace song." You know the one that says, "Let there be peace on earth and let it begin with me." This is how Mother Mary says peace will come to earth. It has to come through our individual lives. It's difficult to describe this special day with mere words. So much is felt, perceived, and given in unseen ways. Mother Mary's presence was so powerful.*

*I apologize to the lady who wrote us to say she was disappointed that the events of August 15th were not in the August newsletter. Maybe I need to tell you how we go about putting the newsletter together. Usually I write my part toward the end of odd numbered months. For August, Byron and I wrote our part the last week of July. We correct each other's work to the best of our ability. Then we wait for Mother Mary to give Her message. So to write about an event that is to happen in the future is impossible. Byron puts the newsletter into the format you receive. After that, we fax it to our publisher who corrects any typos or grammatical errors. It is corrected and sent to a local printer. We then label, stamp, and stuff the envelopes. We work at this as fast as we can so that you receive your newsletter as quickly as we can get it to you, usually about the middle of the month. I hope this clears up any misconceptions.*

*I've been trying to think of what I'm learning or working on now. I seem to be in a period of rest. After the open house I went to Dallas to work with my therapist and that seemed to help me complete a lot of the inner work that had me toiling away for months. It feels good to have gotten back to a state of inner peace and serenity. I've been working on abuse issues for fifteen years and have finally brought sweet closure to it all.*

*I'm not going to think that "I've got It" now—not by a long shot. It feels good to know that the most painful part is over. I remind myself that I'm still living and breathing here on earth, in a very human existence. In the words of Gilda Radner, "It's always something." So I expect that I will be back into expanding what I know by living Mother Mary's messages. But for now this is a time of great gratitude. Isn't that appropriate, just as we are getting close to Thanksgiving.*

*Well, until next time, I remain your friend. —annie*

❖ ❖ ❖

My Dear Children, I come to you with a peaceful yet concerned heart. I am pleased that so many are heeding my call to pray. It is so very important in your individual lives. Each day begin your day in prayer and end your evening in prayer. It is so very important that you do this—I cannot stress it too much. There are so many things that happen as you pray. It is an interactive experience. As you open your heart and mind to pray, you also open your heart and mind to God.

He has the opportunity to give you more of His spirit, more of His love, and more of His energy. During your moments of prayer, there is so much happening in the unseen levels of your life. You may think that you live only the outer physical life where you see with your eye, hear with your ears, and feel with your body. But in actuality, there is much that takes place deep within your being. Have you not heard the expression, that a certain person runs deep, or has depth of character? Most often when you question that person, they will tell you they spend time in prayer. God is able to plumb your being and make your life mean so much more. Depth of character happens, and depth of soul and depth of heart and mind takes place as you stay in prayer.

There are small changes taking place in the consciousness of mankind. For each small change that takes place, many prayers are required from many, many different people. This is why it is so important that you pray each day. This is why I return again and again to this request. Only when there are changes in individual people's lives can there be changes in mankind's consciousness. Each time you pray, each time our thought turns towards all that is good, loving, and peaceful, you are making a difference. This is why I'm asking each of you to observe a day of prayer. To set aside one day a month to think, feel, and pray for peace. I request that you observe this day on the 15th of every month.

But allow yourself to be flexible, and if this is not a good day or you forget, do not berate yourself; simply make the next available day your day of prayer. I've said many times before that prayer is talking to God. Can you not spend one whole day speaking to God about all the things that concern you, worry you, or puzzle you? Can you not ask God's blessings on the people you know and love? Do you not have the compassion in your heart to be concerned for the homeless, the dying, the children, those who are suffering from the effects of natural disaster? Can you not remember the people who are still living with abuse or addiction in their lives? Are you not concerned about your governments? Can you not have concern for the people who are living with chronic diseases and handicaps?

Pray for the economy of your world. Pray for schools and teachers, as they have a great responsibility to teach the children not only the lessons, but how to live as they go about their day. Pray for your medical personnel and for all scientists that they may use their integrity and know-how to help people, and not just themselves. Pray for every phase of life. Churches and church leaders need your prayers, that they may have tolerance and an open mind. Pray for the different factions that are opposed to freedom of thought, freedom to worship God.

My little children, you have been making a difference with your prayers. It is not time that you rest from praying. It is time to increase your prayers. Pray with fervor and good sentiments. This is the best way to help yourself, your family, and your nation. It is the best and highest good you can offer not only yourself and your loved ones, but humanity. Just as your body is made up of individual cells, so is humanity made up of individual people. When one part of your body becomes infested with disease, or injury, the whole body suffers. This is what happens to humanity and mankind. But also, just as a fairly healthy body can recuperate easier than one that is not in good health, so humanity recuperates as more and more people become spiritually healthy. Your prayers help you to maintain your spiritual health.

Do not pay attention to the news media. They love to focus on the scandals and the violence. Seldom do they let you know of the many people who care for others, the animals, or the planet. Most stories are told in such a way to leave doubt as to what the good people are doing. When you give credence to these types of stories, you are looking at appearances. My son, Jesus, told you two thousand years ago not to look at appearances. What he was saying is not to look at the face value of anything, but look beyond the first presentation. He cautioned you to seek the truth in all things.

When you think of your prayers, infuse them with your faith. You have much to be joyful about, and your faith is only one of the aspects of your soul that increases as you pray. Remember that Jesus often said to the people who came to be healed, "It will be done according to your faith." The more you pray, the more, you become serene and peaceful. There is no greater force or power than God's, and in your prayers you are infused with this great force and power. It is the constant communication with this great Source of Goodness, Energy, Intelligence, and Wholeness that happens when you pray to a loving and caring God.

Too many people still pray with fear in their hearts, because they still believe in a vengeful and angry God. In this belief is the concept that you could be harmed by God. The real Truth is that God is more like a loving parent to his only child. The only begotten child of God is humanity. So as you heal the remnants of anger, fear, envies, resentments, and grievances in your heart, you help heal humanity of its woes. You are doing good, so continue to pray.

One of the reasons I've requested that you set aside the 15th of the month for praying for peace, is that prayers are accumulative, and so when a large group focuses their prayers on peace at approximately the same time period, you do great work for mankind and humanity. Please do all you can to comply with this request. If for any reason it is impossible, then pledge to pray daily for peace. All prayers are good. Simply talk to God, let Him hear your concerns, worries, needs, and wants. Speak to Him as you would to a loving Father or Mother. You can certainly do your part to move mankind and you into the Thousand Years of Peace. I thank you for heeding my request and am loving each of you dearly.

Mary, Mother of Jesus.

# The Birth of Christ

12/99

*Here we are again in the Holiday Season. During this Thanksgiving I've been thanking God for each of you. I would still do this work because I do it for God, and because I love being Mary's messenger. But you are like the icing on the cake and being Mary's messenger is the cake. I love receiving your letters, calls, and e-mails. I apologize for not answering them all. I have no excuse; writing letters has never been my strong suit. Now isn't this ironic? It seems that God uses the things I don't like as well as the things I do. The fact that I will do almost anything before I write a letter has always been Byron's way of "knowing" that it isn't me doing the work when it comes to getting the messages.*

*So what am I learning right now? I'm learning that I can learn a lesson, like unconditional love, over and over, and still receive new revelations, new insights. It seems to be a subject that just keeps growing and growing. I've often heard Mother Mary talk about our "heart of hearts." And I thought I understood it, but it seems that now I have a better understanding of what She is talking about.*

*As many of you know, we have had a few family challenges this year. What Mother Mary taught me in the past few weeks is that when I love unconditionally, I love from my heart of hearts. Our heart of hearts never gets broken, is never injured in any way, because it never judges. Our heart gets broken, is disappointed, feels betrayed, and hurts. It is in our heart that we feel guilty, remorseful, angry, fearful, and all depleting emotions. But our heart of heart just loves.*

*It's nice to have two hearts, especially when you are not feeling so nice; and to know that the one that holds nasty emotions can feel unconditional love, but that there is another, much deeper heart that has always remained pure, clean, and loving. Sometimes we think we've been feeling unconditional love, and then something happens and we feel angry, hurt, and other depleting emotions, and we wonder what happened. It's then that we can remind ourselves that we have another, deeper heart that doesn't feel these depleting emotions. It reminds us that we are spiritual, but while on earth we are also human. When someone hurts us, either intentionally or unintentionally, and we feel strong emotions—we can't help it; it's part of our humanness. So I'm learning to appreciate my humanness.*

*We talk a lot about love during Christmas, and we buy each other gifts trying to express that love. But to me the way we best express love is to keep loving our family members and friends even when they are not acting out of love—even when they are acting out of their pain, fear, anger, or greed. This is when we truly love unconditionally. Often in talks I've given around the country, I get very specific and relate an incident or two, and will say that this person is in my life to teach me to love unconditionally. I wish I could say that I've mastered loving unconditionally, but it's something I'm still working on. It may take me a lifetime to learn.*

*Once again I relearned that I am to love myself unconditionally, that harsh self-judgment is futile and useless. It gets me no where fast. I'm reminded that I'm responsible for myself first. It's up to me to be sure that my needs are being met. It's up to me to set boundaries and then to honor those boundaries. If I take care of myself, I free my loved ones from this responsibility, and then they are free to be themselves. All of this is part of loving myself.*

*But most of all, I think that Christmas makes us realize how important it is to honor our loved ones and their needs and bound-*

aries. It reminds us that, although we can't make another person happy if they don't want to be, we can love them by honoring who they are and how they choose to live their life.

Recently, the Brotherhood gave a message in which they spoke of our family. They were not talking about our parents, siblings, children and such, but of our human family. In Mary's Message to the World, *Mother Mary said that every race is our brother and every religion is our sister. She also said that to accept and appreciate is to love.* I think we come closer to this being true at Christmas than at any other time of the year. So maybe this is where it all starts, simply with acceptance.

In the book Mother Mary asked us to accept our differences and similarities. So how many of us have accepted the differences in ourselves and our spouses . . . or the differences in ourselves and our siblings? It's something to think about. But then there is the other side of this. How many of our family have accepted the differences in us? Not only do we have to accept the differences that lie between us and our family, but we have to accept that sometimes family and acquaintances do not accept the things that make us different from them.

It's a simple matter of how much do we want to love? How much do we want peace in our lives? How far are we willing to go to maintain self-esteem and inner peace? I know that as I've come to accept the things that make me different from everyone else, the easier it's been to accept the differences in others. I find the differences intriguing and interesting. But my New Year's resolution is to do all I can to set aside my biases and prejudices.

I hope you have a very, very happy Holiday Season, that you and your family are safe, find the Spirit of Christmas and have a Joyful Christmas, a loving Christmas, and a peaceful Christmas. May your new year and new millennium be filled with only wonderful, good experiences and a continuation of this Holiday's Spirit. Until next time I remain your friend. —annie

✧ ✧ ✧

# THE BIRTH OF CHRIST

My Dear Children, I come to you in understanding, peace, and joy. Once again you on earth are celebrating the birth of Jesus. But remember that this celebration is but a remembrance of the birth of the Christ Child within each person. The story of Jesus' birth was true but can also be used as an analogy. Within each person is the child of God. The child of God is created in God's image and likeness. As God is spirit, so are you. As God is total goodness, so are you, when you seek within to find that place that my son, Jesus, called the "kingdom of heaven."

Jesus' birth fulfilled many of the old prophesies. His birth represented the coming of the new. He brought with him light. In the beginning God created light. But Jesus brought light in stronger and in newer ways. He said many times, "I am the light of the world, ye are the light of the world." Not only was he the light of the world, but you each bring with you a light that only leaves this body when the soul leaves. Each of you have a light that you are to let shine. But you cannot let your light shine if your heart and mind are steeped in hatred, biases, prejudices, greed, anger, and fear. Your light will not shine when you allow your human self to puff up with your own importance, or when you begin to think that you are better than another person. All people, no matter the color of their skin, were created by God. Every person is part of the human race, and the human race is God's child.

Whenever you choose, you can give birth to the Christ child within you. You can become the beloved one of God. It requires that you love God above all else. This means that you love Him above and beyond your beliefs, the teachings of your religions, the preconceived ideas you have concerning God, Spirit, Church, and Creation. It means you love God beyond your own understanding, your own life, your own self. It means that you learn to love yourself with wisdom, and that you love your neighbor as yourself.

I ask that you first learn to love yourself with wisdom so that you will have a good self-concept of who you are and what you value in reality. Then you can fully love your neighbor as yourself in a good way. Your neighbor is not only those who live close to your home, but those who live on this planet. Begin to see that every person on this earth is your neighbor. Finding within your heart the ability to accept them is a good place to start. Acceptance is love in action, in accepting the beauty of the differences in skin color, tradition, culture, values, and in people that you love.

Accepting loved ones, friends, acquaintances, and people just as they are is loving unconditionally. To accept that loved ones don't always agree with you, or that friends may not see from your perspective, is loving without judgment. Accepting people without trying to change or correct them is loving in God's way. And what can be more beautiful, more energizing, than to love as God does? It energizes you because you are no longer responsible to monitor or watch others to see that they do what is "right." You no longer have to be vigilant over what you have no control over in the first place. It energizes the person you truly accept so that he/she is free to act and react according to their own inner self. They no longer need to be vigilant to act or react according to your specifications. They are free, and you are free on many levels.

Acceptance is the first step towards peace. You must be accepting of differences and accepting of the innate goodness that is within the human spirit in order to begin to settle issues, to negotiate disagreements, to bring peaceful resolution to war. So during this holiday season, recalling a time

# THE BIRTH OF CHRIST

when the angels sang "Peace on Earth, goodwill to men," I ask that you make a commitment to accept yourself just as you are, accept your loved ones, and accept your fellow humans just as they are.

This is a time of joy, and joy comes to those who are free to love as God loves. Joy is more than contentment; it is more than happiness, it is alive, energizing, and edifying. Joy itself brings peace, love, and understanding. "Joy to the World" you sing each Christmas, but how can there be joy when there is suffering? How can there be joy when you still harbor resentments, unresolved angers, and when many people terrorize each other? How can you have a joyful time when children are still being brutalized in many parts of the world? How can there be joy when you still judge each other harshly?

Joy lives in an atmosphere of peace, love, and understanding. I would have each of you realize that the greatest joy you can have is to clear from your heart depleting emotions. The greatest gift you can give each other is to pray the one for the other with love. Revitalize your relationships with joyfulness and understanding. It takes tolerance, patience, and compassion to have the great joy that brought the angels out to sing that night Jesus was born.

Tolerance is an attribute that will help you have not only joy, but will help you to love without judgment and to set aside your prejudices. Tolerance allows you to see the similarities between you and others of different races, different cultures, and different countries. Tolerance soothes the need to judge. It gives you the understanding to seek ways to find compromise.

Understanding gives you the wisdom to find peace in your mind, heart, and inner self. Understanding opens within your mind, and you receive new insight into old problems, a new perspective into old judgments and comprehension. To fully understand another person is to comprehend his circumstances, situations, background, intellect, and culture.

Compassion is what you feel during this time of Christmas as you prepare to help the needy, the downtrodden, and the helpless. Compassion, along with tolerance and understanding, is what I request that you keep in your heart and mind throughout the new year, and take with you into the new millennium.

Let the birth of Jesus remind you that his way was the way of love, forbearance, tolerance, understanding, and compassion. The remembering will allow you to live each day as your life unfolds into joy, love, and peace. Let this be your new goal in life, your new attitude, and your new way of living.

Thank you for listening to my words. I love each of you greatly.

Mary, Mother of Jesus.

# 50

## A Time of Change

2/2000

CAN YOU BELIEVE THAT WE ARE IN A NEW CENTURY, *much less a new millennium? It's hard for me to believe I've lived this long. In the 1950s and 1960s I thought the year 2000 was way off in the future. I also thought I wouldn't live that long. And here I am alive and well in the year 2000. I'm not sure if I'm elated or disappointed. Either way, I get to continue to live and live and live some more.*

*I received a couple of things about this year I would like to share with you. One is that this is a year of transition—that the changes (earth changes, I think) will not go into effect until next year. I thought this was interesting since many have been saying that according to the Gregorian calendar the new millennium doesn't begin until next year.*

*The other thing was a question. "What do you want to leave in the last century and what is it that you want to take with you into the new century?" It wasn't until I was asked this question that I thought about the century. I had heard so much about the new millennium, and had talked about it that way, that I hadn't even thought about a new century. A millennium is an abstract term for me. I have had a difficult time with the concept of a 1000 years. But a century is something I can fathom.*

*My dad was born in 1892 and my maternal grandmother was also born around that time. They were very near the same age. So my whole life I've had the impression of a century. I used to ask both my dad and my grandmother about the last century. I thought it was so neat to have been around that long. Now here I am living that same experience and not feeling at all old.*

*So the question made me think. I knew one thing I wanted to leave behind was pain and illness. During the holiday season I stopped off at one of the health food stores to buy some supplements and found a new product that has all but taken my pain away. I now have energy and enthusiasm. I hope and pray that I have truly left pain and illness behind me.*

*One other thing I wanted to leave behind was whatever poverty consciousness I still had in effect in my life. Needless to say there are many other things that make up my list. What has happened is that, when I find myself beginning to think in a poverty way or to feel an ache, I deny it. I've been giving myself pep talks and doing affirmations to eliminate what I don't want to live with in this century, and the rest of my life on earth.*

*Then of course, I get to decide what I do want and how I want to live out the rest of my life in this new century. I think back to all the changes that happened soon after 1900. Think about it! The changes were quite dramatic. I feel that in my life I want that kind of permanent good change to happen in my life experience. But I must work on it from the inside first before it will happen on the outside. I recall Mother Mary's words concerning my son David coming to our family meetings with his beer. She said we would "change the inside and then the outside would take care of itself."*

*How many times do we want to make changes in our lives and start to make the changes consciously? We want to change the way we talk, walk, relate to people, how we look, and so on. The first thing we women do when we want to change is either get a new hairdo or get new clothes. What we need to change is something on the inside. So as you begin to live in this new century, remember that if we change the inside, the outside will take care of itself. I'm working hard to change my thought patterns and my feelings. I'm monitoring myself closely to make sure that how I'm living on the inside is how I want to live on the outside.*

*There is a definite correlation here. David is proof of the benefits of starting from the inside. One year after we began to meet as a family to pray and meditate, he went into a rehab hospital and has been in recovery ever since. He celebrated ten years of sobriety last year. He reminds me that he is sober one day at a time. He makes no promises about tomorrow, and it has worked. He changed the inside and the outside took care of itself.*

*I'm still not sure what this year will bring as a direction for me. But one thing that Mother Mary asked is to make myself available once a month. She also asked that I open my home at that time to people. So beginning in February, the second Saturday, I will be available to anyone who cares to visit. We will meditate and pray, probably discuss topics of interest, and I will share what I'm receiving. We will learn together whatever Spirit wants to teach us.*

*For the last couple of years I've been praying to be able to do the things that Jesus did. Remember, he said that the things he did we would do and greater things. Mother Mary says that Jesus came to demonstrate our full potential. I'm hoping that together we will begin to realize our full potential, not to be better than anyone else, or to be other people's savior, but to honor God's great hope for us. So this is an open invitation.*

*I would love to have you join me in praying for the names in our prayer basket. We can make great differences in people's lives with our prayers. Mother Mary has told us that to pray for others is the greatest and best gift we can give. So please join me in praying for the names in our prayer basket. We don't have to know what to pray for. I simply support each person in their own prayers. What they ask for is between them and God. I believe my role is to sustain them with my faith, and that God gives us only that which is good . . . always.*

*So now it's on to everyday living. I hope we all have a great year 2000! Until next time I remain your friend. —annie*

◇ ◇ ◇

My Dear Children, I come in joy and love. It is a great privilege to bring to you words of encouragement, words of instruction, and words to make your life enjoyable. You are living in a wonderful time, a time of great change. It is soon upon you, these great changes. While in reality the changes have been going on for several years, it is just now becoming noticeable to your scientists and other learned ones. You will hear of changing weather patterns, changes in climate, and of changes in many other areas. The migration of birds will be affected, as will the ocean currents. The migration and ocean currents will be talked about in a very short time.

I would have you be prepared to meet any eventuality. When you are prepared, both physically and spiritually, as you can be, I would have you enjoy a peaceful life. I would have you enjoy the changes, enjoy the times you live in. When you enjoy, you are truly experiencing life. Take delight in your daily activities. Let the thoughts and meditations of your mind be upon goodness, joy, love, and most definitely peace. This is how to live in these days.

Many of you will have challenges, but in every challenge you will find goodness, and in that goodness you will find blessings. Let your attitude be one of peaceful enjoyment, and you will find that your daily life is more serene. Meet the challenges that come to you with equanimity. Then you will hear the inner voice that guides you in all things. Look within for your guidance, my children. Listen well as God speaks to you in a silent voice. But this silent voice is heard and recognized when you pay attention to your inner self.

When you can hear the silent voice of God within you, you will have peace and joy. There is nothing like relying and trusting God to protect, supply your every need, and to love you. Right now you are living on faith, but, my little children, that is exactly how you are to live every day. Faith is the substance of all your tomorrows. In the years to come you will still have many harsh realities to face. It will require you to be strong in faith and to trust completely. It will not be difficult to face whatever is in the future with a strong connection to God. Let your heart be at peace for this is why you live. You live to be strongly connected to God and to enjoy the life He has given you. You live to have choices and to make use of your gift of choice. You live to love freely, without encumbrances of judgment or biases.

As you begin your meditations, state your intention. Let each meditation have at least one specific intention, and you may have other intentions. My children, God hears your heart of hearts and understands you fully. Because He has given you freedom of choice, you must ask for what you want. It is your choice to be connected to Him, to have His help as you learn to trust and depend upon Him. There is nothing you cannot ask of God. I must warn you though, God will give only that which is for your highest good and the good of the whole.

In order to trust, you will need to have the belief that God is reliable and that God can be trusted with your best interest. If you believe God is capricious and changeable, you will not be able to trust Him completely. I have said that God loves each of you unconditionally over and over. When you hold this truth deep within your core beliefs, you will be able to trust.

A portion of trust is the anticipation and confidence that what you ask for is done. If you will remember when my son, Jesus, prayed, he thanked God for the answer immediately. It was a part of the asking. Ask from your deepest longings. Ask for what is the best and highest for you. Let God hear your request. Then anticipate the answer. Then stand back and watch as God works wonders in your life.

Remember that at times God must prepare you to receive what you long for. Many times you are not ready to receive your answer. Then there are others to consider and their good must be taken into account too. Most often, it takes time for all of this to happen. So as you wait and anticipate, increase your faith and your trust through affirmations. Anticipate the answer enough to be grateful for the answer before it gets to you. Daily be grateful that all your prayers are answered in surprising and wondrous ways. Remember, God can accomplish a deed in the twinkling of an eye. But many times this is not what is best for you. Therefore the wait is part of the preparation for you to be able to receive.

Enjoy the wait. Take pleasure in the anticipation of the answer. Never dictate to God how it must come. If you think you would never dictate to God, you do when you hold preconceived ideas of how an answer is to be given. When you tell God in your prayers what is needed, you dictate. You are only to ask and wait for the answer. Your answer will come in God's own good time and in His own good way. Simply wait and trust. Yes, my children, it is simple but not always easy.

Open yourself up to receive, however the answer comes. Many times you delay the answer to your prayer because you want it to be given in a certain way and to look like what you think it should. In whatever manner God answers your prayer it will be good, because God only gives good. You must believe this with all your heart, all your mind, and all that you are. Begin today to believe in the goodness of God, in His Divine Love, and in His great compassion. Believe that

God wants you to enjoy life and not to suffer through it. Believe that God wants there to be peace in your life, in your world, and in your future. Jesus believed in a God who loved you so much He would withhold nothing from you except that which would cause you harm. Focus all your attention, all your concentration, and all your being on the goodness of God, on His love, and on His peace. You can do this, my children; it is well within your ability to change your belief from a God who punishes to one who loves unconditionally, who gives only good to His children.

Use these messages to better your life. Use them daily to change your world. There can be peace and enjoyment of life. I love each of you.

Mary, Mother of Jesus.

# The Power of Resurrection

4/2000

I FEEL THAT I AM IN THE EBB—*not always a fun place to be but one that is so much a part of life on earth. Many years ago the Brotherhood told us that all things on earth flow just like the tides, in an ebb and flow pattern.*

*The ebb is different from the void, which is even more uncomfortable, and for me can last longer. In the ebb everything seems to be moving as slow as molasses. When I look at my spiritual development it seems that nothing much is happening. Emotionally I feel like I'm not feeling. Mentally it feels like I stopped thinking. But the inner messages still come through. I just don't seem to have the wonder, the awe that is so exciting.*

*I've been hearing a little song, in my mind, that my friend Anita led us in at the second "Earth Festival" (1996) during an unscheduled break. She tells me that John Denver sang it on a children's tape he made. The words are something like this. "It is within each of us to be wise. Look within. Open up both your eyes. You can do anything without even knowing how. It is within each of us. Here and now." I hope the words are correct. If not, this is the message I'm getting.*

*When I look back at this whole journey with my spiritual awakening, the visits from Mother Mary, and Her request to me—I didn't know what I was doing then. I was good at following* directions. I've been reminding God that I'm not getting the message if He is sending it, because I don't know what to do or how to do it. Maybe the song is God telling me I don't have to know how. Once again I'm reminded to look within, where wisdom and knowledge are. All we have to do is look within. So simple, but not always easy.

I think it's a matter of trust. Do I trust God—to care for me, to be there when I need Him, to show me the way, to be all things for me? My first reaction to this question is, of course I do! But if I trust—then why all the questioning and fretfulness? Maybe I must trust myself first. Do I trust myself, or maybe the question is, CAN I trust myself? Sometimes I think I can, and at other times it seems that I just don't.

The words of the song keep repeating themselves to me, "You can do anything without even knowing how." And I have seen such a beautiful example of someone who actually lives these lines. She is the sister of my good friend, Anita. For some time now she has been listening to her inner guidance and simply following the instructions. She began to create sculptures and is now painting on canvas. The work is beautiful, inspiring, and mind provoking. When I think of doing anything without even knowing how, she inspires me.

I've often asked why I need to learn old lessons over and over. I'm told that I'm learning it on different levels. Don't you often know something in your mind but haven't learned it yet in your heart? I'm a little slow and so it takes me a while to learn a lesson. Then I'm easily bored, and so they give me a break in the repeated lessons. Sometimes it's so long that I forget I've already learned this once. And so it's like learning once again for the first time. So here goes the lesson on trust once again, and I hope I get it this time.

I feel it's giving myself permission to trust myself. In my past I've not been good at taking care of me. For years I was gullible and didn't try to use logic, reason, or any thinking process to make choices. I just went along never really making a choice, but being led through indecision. What I've learned through therapy is that the trust, that should have been there for me as a child, was not. So I didn't learn how to trust and now am learning and relearning that I can trust me.

*I still feel like we are in the ebb. Byron and I are in a deep ebb in some areas of our lives. But the good thing about being in the ebb is that soon we will be back into the flow again. One other thing that has come through for me that you may relate to—since the first of the year we have been in a financial ebb. I asked why is this happening when I firmly believe that God is my Source. The answer was that I still hold a belief in good and evil.*

*When I first began to seek, I asked to know God's Truth. I wanted to know what was really, really true, even if it was different than the commonly held beliefs. I remembered that once people believed the Earth was flat, but God knew it was round. He simply waited for us to find out the real truth. What Mother Mary has taught me is that in God's Realm and Truth there is no evil. God is not fighting some evil spirit for our souls. He is simply waiting for us to find out the truth that all the evil in the world is our own creation.*

*So how does this affect our finances? It seems that part of the belief in good and evil is the belief in feast or famine. So as long as I believe in feast or famine, I will experience these events in my life. Now I'm affirming that the real truth is that in God there is only goodness, love, health, and abundance. I can experience this when I change my beliefs. So in light of these lessons I am now practicing— I am confident that I will experience the flow again, learn to trust myself, and experience abundance everyday. I don't have to know how. All I have to do is look inside just as the song says. It's the same lesson over and over until I get it. Jesus taught us this when he said, "It's the Father within who does the work." All I have to do is get my personality and ego out of the way and allow Him to work through me. Then I can do anything, even if I don't know how. Something to think about isn't it? I hope you all are doing well. It is my prayer that you have only God's goodness in your lives every day. Until next time, I remain your friend. —annie*

◇ ◇ ◇

# THE POWER OF RESURRECTION

My Dear Children, it is with great joy that I come to you once again at this time of renewal. This is the time to celebrate life and the continuation of life. When you look at Jesus' death, concentrate on his resurrection. For in his resurrection is the story of life. Death is simply a part of the on-going saga of life. Life is beautiful, just the simple act of living is beautiful.

While you are on earth, to live is to keep body and soul together. But I would have you do more than this. I request that you keep your concentration on keeping your body and soul infused with your spirit. It is the spirit of God that animates you. He is your life force, He is the power that gives you life. Many times people lose their spirit in life. Then they just exist. They lose the joy in life. To lose your spirit is to lose your enthusiasm for life. When you lose your spirit you also lose your zest for life and the activities in your life.

This is a time of renewal in nature and it can be the time for restoring your spirit's connection to your soul and your body. You can resurrect your spirit's life force. You can rehabilitate your life through your mind and heart. It takes both the mind and the heart to accomplish the rehabilitation. First you make the decision to rehabilitate your life. Then your desire for a better life connects decision and desire to bring you to accomplishment. This is true for all kinds of rehabilitation. You can rehabilitate your mind by cleansing it from depleting thoughts, attitudes, and beliefs. In this way you can rehabilitate your heart from depleting and spirit-robbing emotions.

When you rehabilitate and renew your life in this way, you are truly using the power of resurrection to restore your life force. The power of resurrection is demonstrated at this time of year through nature. That which had been dormant and looked dead is revitalized; it comes to life and not only comes to life but blooms in a profusion of innate beauty. When you go through a period of dormancy, and you feel nothing is happening, just realize that you are in this type of period. In this period of inner rest you may feel that you are not progressing. It is a time for you to allow yourself to catch up on all levels. It is a time to put into practice that which you are learning. It is a time of trusting that you are still very much alive, and that life continues.

The resurrection periods in your life are wonderful. You do not need to await a special season. You can resurrect any part of your life at any time. To resurrect is to refresh, to re-energize and to rebuild. God is willing and able to help you do this. He will not do it for you, but He will work with you and through you to reestablish a strong inner connection to Him. When you have more of God in your life, you have more vital, energizing, original life force flowing through you. In all things allow God to help you.

If you have an addiction, let God help you set it aside. It is not always an easy thing to do. With God's power and help you can let any addiction go. If you have a contentious nature and find that you are more willing to see the wickedness in people or situations, be restored through God's love. If you have a dour and downhearted outlook on life, be revived through God's joy. If you find that you are filled with guilt and shame, be regenerated through God's forgiving and loving nature. If you are overcome with fears and terrors, be rejuvenated through God's understanding and strength.

In God you will find all goodness. Not one of His attributes is denied you. When you think you can't cope and need courage, He is with you. When you feel fearful and weak, His strength is there. When you are lonely and despairing, His love surrounds you. When you are angry and overcome with dark emotions, God's peace and love are with you. When you feel guilty and ashamed, God's forgiveness is true. When you are fretful and filled with resentments, God's serenity enfolds you. When you feel disconnected from life, His presence hugs you. When you grieve, God comforts you. When you are filled with sadness and confusion, He will sustain you with His love. In every condition God is with you. In every circumstance and situation God will infuse you with His goodness.

God will never abandon you or neglect you. But He will not impose His will upon you, for to do so would negate His gift of freedom of choice. He simply waits for you to seek Him. He waits for you to ask, that is why Jesus was so sure that God would be with you that he said, "Ask and it shall be given unto you, seek and you shall find, knock and it shall be opened." If you will look closely, you will see that he didn't say it may or it could be; Jesus was so certain and trusting that he didn't equivocate or put any conditions on this promise. God is that infallible, that dependable, and that trustworthy. God will not fail you, my children. He loves each of you too much.

To resurrect your life, put more spirit into your life. Resurrect your prayer and meditation time. Resurrect your faith in God. You can transform your life through the power of resurrection. But only you can do this. It requires that you make the decision and the deep commitment to yourself and to God. You will need to be open and honest with yourself. But I have full faith in the goodness of God and in the ability of people to transform and to renew. I have full faith in the trustworthiness of God to help you in every way, as long as you make the effort to do your part.

Enjoy this season and let it speak to your soul. Spring and the blossoming forth of nature will tell you that life is eternal. That although things change, it also stays the same. That life will not be denied its time of renewal. That life can be restored and that you can rehabilitate any part of your life. Be quiet and let the power of the resurrection take place in you. Renew your prayers with more dedication. Refresh your meditation with more faithfulness. Revitalize your heart through forgiveness. Re-energize your body with your good thoughts. Reorganize your mind through a belief in God's love. You are eternal, spiritual beings. You are children of a benevolent Creator. Let this soothe your soul.

Mary, Mother of Jesus.

# 52

## Truth Clears the Way

*6/2000*

THE LAST NEWSLETTER SEEMED TO HAVE STRUCK A CORD with many of you. I heard from quite a few people who either felt the same ebb, felt the need to cheer me up, or simply to give me their view of the ebb. Thank you all for responding; it's always comforting to know that someone out there understands. It's also comforting to know there are friends who are in this human experience with me.

Do I still feel the ebb? I feel a change more than an ebb now. While I was in New Jersey this past month, I commented on feeling a change coming. It feels like I'm waiting and not knowing what I'm waiting for. Many of the participants in the workshop were feeling a change coming in their lives, too. Mother Mary said this is a year of transition; I feel it's not a calendar year but a period of time. I think the "year" began maybe last fall and will continue through the spring of 2001.

It feels like a time of preparation, but I'm not sure how to prepare. I know that, most of the time, preparation, for me, means more prayer and more meditation. It means scrutinizing my inner self to see what needs to be cleared away. My meditation time has fallen by the wayside over the past few years. I used to meditate for hours at a time. Now I do thirty or forty minutes. When I think of how much time I used to spend in meditation, it seems that now I'm slacking off, even though I still meditate daily. Also I've been falling asleep during my meditations, which is frustrating. In our family meetings, I learned that if I start with a statement of intention, the intention is what happens during my meditation.

As an example: usually my intention is to strengthen my connection to God, or to be in God's presence, or to simply commune with God. If I fall asleep, the Brotherhood assures me that it's only my conscious mind that sleeps. My spirit, my soul, carries out my request to be with God. But being the human being that I am, I like to be conscious and aware during my meditations. I like the feeling of having accomplished a meditation according to my idea of how a meditation should go. AND . . . yes, I do know that "shoulds" are a "no-no," and never help you feel good about yourself.

Well, I'm preparing as best I can, which were Mother Mary's exact words to me many years ago. Once when I asked her how to do what she requested, she replied, "Do it as best you can." I'm also beginning to look forward to the transformation that's taking place within me to be completed. I can feel the transformation taking place, but I'm not sure what all, or what areas, are transforming.

Lately, I've been asking, what am I learning? I'm told the lesson is on trust and that this will be one of the things I work on this year and throughout this life experience. I thought I'd already learned to trust, but I'm told I missed some of the finer points. Now I have the opportunity to concentrate on them, again. It's true that trusting hasn't been easy for me. I thought it had more to do with my childhood abuse experiences and issues. In the past, people I thought I could trust, betrayed me. I married at sixteen before I had developed any real self-confidence or trust. When I married my first husband, he didn't live up to his marriage vows. It was the old betrayal and trust issue again, but in a different guise, and with a different person. I'm convinced that, if we don't learn our lessons the first time, they keep coming back through different people and different circumstances. Many times in talks I say, "Don't worry if you don't get 'it' the first time, God will give many opportunities to do so."

If we haven't learned what we can from our family of origin, we will marry a person who will give us opportunities to learn the *lesson, or work for someone who will personify the issue, or live next door to someone, or be friends with people who will bring the lesson to us over and over again, until we get "it."* So I married the perfect person at a very young age to bring the issue of trust into my life and to have it sit in my face for over twenty years. At the time I wasn't aware of the opportunity; it felt like betrayal, and it reinforced the thought that I couldn't trust anyone, not even myself. But in reality, I was learning all I could about trust by experiencing the absence of trust.

So what have I learned about trust? For me it's more about learning to trust my own instincts and reactions. Learning to trust the information that comes to me, for me, and about me. Also, I've learned that trust is a skill. It gets better the more you rely upon it or rely upon yourself. When I looked up the word "trust" in the dictionary, I found that it was about having confidence, depending, believing, hoping, and having faith. In the past, I hadn't been able to depend upon myself. The circumstances of my life choices didn't leave me with many opportunities to learn to be independent. And being a true-blue, raging, co-dependent, I was afraid of being independent. So I've had to learn to have faith in myself, to believe in myself, and be self-confident. I'm still practicing these things. I thought they were separate lessons. By looking the word "trust" up in the dictionary, I found out that these were all the same lessons on trust.

Whatever state I find myself in, I am transforming, changing, and continuing to learn. But then, don't all of us have these same kind of experiences in our lives? Isn't it comforting to know that we have so many similar experiences and lessons in common? Isn't it so very wonderful just how different and personalized our lessons are? I feel that God is so amazingly astounding. He loves each of us so much that He allows us to learn in our own way, in our own time frame, and through simply living our life—daily.

Until next time I remain your friend. —annie

✧ ✧ ✧

My Dear Children, I come to you today in understanding and with a compassionate heart. I call you to open your mind and heart. Allow yourself to open your mind and heart to compassion, courage, and tolerance. It takes a heart filled with compassion to learn to love yourself and others without conditions. It takes a mind filled with courage to make the necessary changes within to live in peace. And it will take wisdom to know when and where to help yourself and others. Tolerance allows you to have compassion without limit, to be courageous without fear. Wisdom gives you the ability to know if help is needed, and when it is just a matter of listening or speaking a word. Remember, every hour lived is the right time for a prayer.

Many of you wish to help others, but do not want to face your own issues or to change your own mind-set. You cannot truly help others if you are filled with the denial of your own issues. You do not truly help others if you are intolerant of others' views, beliefs, circumstances, or life choices. Your help will not be real help, but a way to salve your own heart if you are intolerant of the differences in people.

Look within and find the truth of your own situations and circumstances. So many times you find more ways to avoid the truth of your situations and circumstances, and this does not help. Remember who you are and be true to yourself first. It is when you help yourself, and as you go through the process of finding yourself, that you are free to help others with your whole heart and a clear mind. Seek always to speak the truth to yourself. My little children, do not deceive yourself into believing that which is false. Truth in every situation in life is what will guide you to peace.

# TRUTH CLEARS THE WAY

There is no peace in denial. There is no peace in turmoil. There is no peace in intolerance. There is no peace in judgment. Let me explain, my children. When you live in denial of the truth of the events, circumstances, and choices you have made, you will have doubts about yourself and your choices. In denial there is contradiction, and protestations enter your mind and heart. How can you be peaceful filled with doubts, protestations, and contradictions? How can you see what is best, if you do not see the problem with a clear mind and heart?

Denial leads you to turmoil, which causes you to be confused and disturbed. Confusion and disturbances bring disorder and chaos. The chaos and disorder of the world are caused by a lack of truth and unconditional love. Intolerance causes biases which separate you from each other and closes your heart to compassion. Intolerance also causes you to negate your own pain and the pain of others. It also causes you to withhold or restrain your kindness and mercy.

It is imperative that you become compassionate, tolerant, and that you live in truth. This is the way to bring about the changes necessary to instill peace and serenity in the hearts of mankind. It takes more than thinking about tolerance. It takes living a life of tolerance. First, you will be tolerant of yourself. You will allow that you make mistakes and that other people do too. You will be able to allow each person to have their own opinion and make their own choices without fear of your judgment.

Be truthful when you pray, and pray, not to be heard or thought well of by man, but to be heard by God. Remember that God hears the unspoken prayer as well as the spoken one.

He hears your heart of hearts and knows when you pray with earnestness and sincerity. It is your earnest and sincere prayer that is heard the loudest. Many times you pray one way and feel a different way. Your whole being must agree and be made in truth for the answer to come.

Have you not wondered why the prayer said in desperation at the last minute is most often the one answered the quickest? It is often when you reach your last desperate point that your whole being agrees on what the request is. So often you pray for others and ask God specifically to make changes in the other person that you wish to see in their lives. And often these changes are requested irregardless of what is truthfully needed in the situation. But when you are in desperate situations, then you cut away the debris of falseness, deception, and distortions.

Truth clears the way to live your life in peace. Tolerance and compassion allow you to truly help your fellow man. Truth helps you to be understanding. Only when you can acknowledge the pain or error of your own ways can you be understanding of the errors of others' choices. When you are tolerant, you allow others to make their own choices, to find their own inner guidance, and their own inner connection to God. An open mind and heart are a tolerant mind and a compassionate heart.

Express your compassion in tender and loving ways. Let kindness be the way you relate to each other. You can be honest and kind. You can be tender and strong. You can be supportive of others. You can encourage those who have lost their faith. You can associate one with sympathy. You can commiserate and listen, one to the other.

When you understand each other, you will perceive the truth of your relationship. Listen with an open mind so that you can comprehend each others' predicaments and situations. It will be with a deep understanding which will bring insight in how to help yourself and each other. Open your mind to the fact that each of you have a direct route to the Father within. No one person can be a route for the other to find their inner connection. But one person can support, encourage, and teach others how to go within to find their connection to God. An open mind will allow you to see the similarities and to appreciate the differences in people.

An open heart is what is needed today, so that you can find it within you to be of service to mankind. An open heart will express itself in friendliness and benevolence. You will be ready to be of help when called upon. You will be gentle and gracious. You will allow other people to believe as they choose, to choose what they will, and to make their own decisions. You will teach your children to do the same. Let your whole being act from a perspective of love and leave fear behind. To truly be loving is to be understanding, tolerant, and compassionate. You can do this. You have goodness deep within you. Find it, my little children.

Mary, Mother of Jesus.

# 53

# *Serenity*

8/2000

IN PREPARING FOR AUGUST 15TH, *my inner guidance urged me to add more prayer to my day. In case you're wondering about August 15th, it's that special day when Mother Mary makes an apparition near here. I began to prepare for it about mid-July. Due to the preparations, I've noticed a shift in my mind-set. I've been renewing my statements of faith to remind myself what I believe. I use some of the old familiar creeds I learned in the Methodist Church, then go on to state all that I believe today.*

*It has made me realize just how far I've come and how much nearer I am to complying with Mother Mary's early request to cleanse my heart and mind of depleting emotions of fear and anger. I still get angry, but now it's more like being testy or irritated. I used to go instantly into a rage, but I don't do that anymore. In the past ten years I can only remember raging once, and then with very good reason. I was protecting myself and my family.*

*Fear is something I want to deal with as fast as I can. So renewing my statements of faith has caused me to become very, very grateful to God for all my blessings. One thing I'm grateful for is that I no longer live my life in terror. Fear is still something I can deny, but at least I deal with it in a matter of weeks or months. I used to deny fear so well that it lingered for decades. One of the ways I recognize that there is fear or anger which I'm denying is that my energy level goes down. I fully understand why Mother Mary describes fear and anger as depleting emotions. They really do rob me of energy and vitality.*

*I truly believe in a God who is infinitely loving, not just some of the time, but all the time. I no longer view the events of my life, or the circumstances of my life, as punishments from God. But then, I've not believed that in decades. I remember when my oldest son was born with Down's Syndrome. I can't remember who it was, but a woman told me the reason he was born that way was that it was a punishment from God. I didn't believe it then, any more than I believe it now. He was an answer to many prayers. I prayed for a baby; I got one, and he has been with me for forty-four years. He definitely is one of my biggest blessings.*

*I acknowledge, and am grateful, that I have been more than blessed to have been chosen by Mother Mary to do my small part in her labor of love. One of the best blessings I've received through this work is to have met so many beautiful and wonderful people over the years. Through this work I've became friends with many good people and have had many good times as I've traveled.*

*Because of this work, I've been able to heal old wounds that had kept me in unhappiness, terror, and raging anger. Mother Mary didn't wave a magic wand and heal me—not that I don't think that is possible, it just didn't happen that way. I had to do the work. I was required to dig deep into my heart and mind to bring up painful memories and to forgive what, at times, seemed like the unforgivable. What I've learned is that, in forgiving, I set myself free from the terror, raging anger, and unhappiness.*

*I've been blessed with a good husband, good children, and I think my grandchildren are the best. My great-granddaughters are even better than the best. The down side is living so far from them that we seldom see them. Each one of them has a special place in my heart. Even though we don't always see eye to eye, there is love. I've learned to love myself and them unconditionally. I don't have to like everything they do, or always agree with them, for there to be love among us. Even when there is alienation, there is love. And there is total acceptance. Neither do we have to become doormats to love unconditionally. To love as God loves us, we need to totally accept* ourselves just like we are, and to totally accept our loved ones the same way. Then we will be able to accept people who are different, believe differently, or who don't like us.

One of my statements of faith is that I now believe in God's complete and total acceptance of me and every other person on earth. He accepts me just as I am at this moment in time. This helps dissipate the doubts, guilt, and shame that have been prevalent in my life which could easily overtake my thoughts.

When we reaffirm our faith, we reaffirm ourselves. That's been happening to me through this process. Also, I've been able to see how far I've progressed in my goal to cleanse my heart. I see how I live my life today, as opposed to how I used to live in so much fear. I've also realized how much easier it is to love myself and others when I'm no longer afraid of people. I still have a tendency to hold back, especially in a crowd. It's easier now that I'm not as afraid. Long ago a good friend of mine told me I wasn't afraid of dying, I was afraid of living. She was right. Sometimes living can be difficult; at times it takes guts, but once you've settled issues, come out of denial, and faced what you've been avoiding, life can be so good.

That's the blessing I'm experiencing now—a good life. I still have challenges, I'm still working to eradicate things from my life that no longer serve me. But on the whole, it's a good life, and I am blessed.

In reaffirming what I believe, my faith is increasing. This gives me hope. Hope makes life so much more peaceful and fun. It has renewed my interest in many things. Not all of our problems are solved. But I now have hope that we will solve them, or will learn to cope with them, whichever is best.

Sometimes you just have to sit back and take a look at where you were in order to see how far you've come. Every day we learn so much just by living our life. Invariably, when I've asked what I am supposed to be doing, the answer is "live." As I live my life, and you live your life, with faith in a benevolent Creator, we make changes that affect our world. Our faith in a loving God, in the goodness of God, changes everything.

I really appreciate you. As much as I appreciate my family and love them, there is the niggling thought that, as family, it is almost a *requirement to be supportive of me. Logically my mind tells me that isn't true. You, however, don't have to be in my life and your support, gifts, letters, calls, e-mails are deeply appreciated.*

*Guess I'm done enough rambling, so until next time, I remain your friend. —annie*

✧ ✧ ✧

My Dear Children, I come to you in love and with a hopeful heart. The peace of the world is in your hands. It is determined by how you live your life and how well you live your faith. Believe me when I say that God is a loving God, that His love is abiding, everlasting, and enduring. I would not have you be ignorant of this. When you can believe in God's love, you will cease to believe in anything else.

When you believe in God's love, you will be compassionate, faithful, tolerant, and forgiving. God forgives those who ask for it. He forgives you even when you are steeped in anger. He forgives all manner of things. He requires that you forgive yourself in order for the forgiveness to be complete. So many of you are too unrelenting and ruthless with yourselves. In order to be peaceful, you must be forgiving. In order to be loving, you must be forgiving. Love is forgiving. To love is to forgive. This does not mean that who you forgive is absolved of the consequences of his/her mistakes, or he/she is not required to face his/her mistakes or sins. All of God's children must face their mistakes and all are held accountable. When you forgive you give up your own pain, your own anger, and your intolerance.

Be careful, my children, not to concentrate on looking peaceful on the outside and hold bigotry and hatred in your heart. This is not peaceful at all. It is not in outer appearances that I call you to be peaceful. It is within your heart, your thoughts, your attitudes, your longings, your murmuring, and in your dreams that I call you to be peaceful. I call you to treat yourself with peacefulness, to attend to each other in peaceful ways. I call you to be kind-hearted and patient. I call you to be understanding and to release the old hurts from the past. I call you to be tender with yourself and with your loved ones. Then you will have a peaceful nature, one that will seek naturally to end the inner wars and the inner turmoil. You will have the forebearance to end, resolve, and clear away fear, anger, and all manner of depleting emotions.

Serenity comes from a close personal communication with God in your daily life. Accept that every person has this deep inner connection and that every person is responsible to maintain it. Accept that each person will be held accountable for their mistakes when they come to judgment. I would have you dispose of your own issues, addictions, and resentments within your heart and mind first. Then these things will fall away from your outer life for good. When you concentrate on outer appearances, you have changed that which is destroyable. When you change your inner self, you change that which is long-lasting and eternal. Inner changes are the basis of all outer changes in your life.

Remember, my children, you are more than your body, more than your thoughts, and more than your feelings. What happens in your spirit is what matters. What transpires in your spirit is eternal. What brings your spirit closer to God is what is of value. I call you to live from your spirit, to dwell in deep communion with God. Keep this communion active every day.

Your connection to God will be clear and freer when you have cleansed your heart and mind of old grievances, when you have forgiven yourself for mistakes of the past. Your communion with God will be more effective when you have forgiven your fellow man of his mistakes. Seek to find the peace, love, and hope within yourself. Seek to find the wherewithal to forgive all things. Seek to find serenity by facing the issues of your life with honesty, kindness and understanding.

I would have you live a life free of violence. Too many families are at war. Too many people react in destructive ways. Where there is no forgiveness, there is destruction. In unforgiving states of mind you destroy yourselves and destroy your world. An intolerant person has no empathy or sympathy for his own life and does not respect the lives of others. The end of violence in this world will come when you, one by one, become peaceful and understanding in your hearts, nature, and lives.

Help each other in truly helpful ways. Too many people in the name of God become tyrants, inhospitable and indifferent to the plight of their fellow man. Find ways to be of real help. The highest and best way to help yourself and others is through prayer. So many, especially the aged and ill, despair and think they can do no good on earth. As long as you can pray with your whole mind and heart, you can work wonders. Many of you say I can't help or I don't have the money. I remind you that prayer requires no monetary outflow. Yet with your prayers you can effect great changes in the world.

Pray for peace to come, not only to nations or only to governmental negotiations, but to the hearts of the people who are negotiating and to the hearts of the people in nations who are at war. Wars are not caused by governments alone, but by the people those governments represent. Pray for there to be understanding and a coming together with a commitment to seek peace. Many times governments come together not to seek peace but to seek their own selfish means.

Pray not only for the sick of body, but for the sick of mind, and the sick of heart. Pray for a healing to come to parents, so they may live up to their responsibility with joy. Pray that people who father and mother children will put aside their own selfishness and dedicate themselves to the family they have created. Pray for souls still in the throes of their addictions, that they will have the courage to settle the underlying issues that these addictions hide. Pray for the criminally-minded that may find peace and love in their hearts. Pray for the hungry that they will receive not only food for their bodies, but also food for their souls. Pray for the leaders of the world to have integrity, honesty, and truth in their hearts so that, as they lead, they will do so from a compassionate and peaceful life. Pray that all men on earth will rise up in compassion, in honesty, and in peace. This is my call to you. This is my hope for you. This is my prayer for you.

I am loving you each day. Be peaceful, love yourselves, and live in hope.

Mary, Mother of Jesus.

# Hold on to Hope

10/2000

ONE OF THE NEWSLETTER READERS *wrote asking that I explain the annual August 15th Mary Day. When I was receiving the information that became* Mary's Message to the World, *Mother Mary said, "I will appear in your area on August 15th after the book is published." This was about 1989. Since I didn't know if the material would be published I remember thinking, "Well, all right, we'll see." I continued to receive the information that became the book without giving it further thought.*

*The morning of August 15, 1991, a young man, who had read* Mary's Message to the World, *came to our door saying he wanted to stay with me that day in case Mother Mary appeared. I had not had any indication that She would appear, and didn't know what else to do, but welcomed him into our home. If my memory is correct, we had five or six people show up at our door unexpectedly. The only request Mother Mary made was for me to pray every hour. I interpreted that to mean I was to pray for a few minutes every hour ... which is what I did.*

*The next year, I received a very cryptic message, and with the help of a lovely lady in California, deciphered it to mean that we were to go to Joe Pool Lake near Dallas at sunset. About one hundred people joined us that year. That was the year we began publishing the Newsletter to get Her messages out to people per Her request. In the beginning she would say, "It is time to send a message to my readers." So, for that reason, in my heart and soul, you are "Her readers" and not mine. Every year since then we have met by the shores of a lake at sunset on August 15th. In 1996, after we moved to Oklahoma, She said, "Go to the lake nearest you." To me that meant that on August 15th we were to go to Lake Tenkiller.*

*Each year she has appeared to me, not so much as a person, but as an image in the sky. She appears as the form and shape of the standing Madonna. I don't really see eyes, nose, or mouth, but there are shadows that indicate where they are. Inside the Madonna shape is filled with tones of teal blue. The tones give the shape its dimension and indicate a veil and robe. The face and hands are peachy tones. All around her the sky fills with a beautiful pink, that shimmers and twinkles.*

*Each year someone, and often many others, see Her too. Before August of 1992, I'd requested that She please appear to other people at the same time. I was concerned that, if I was the only one to see Her, it could be discounted. In 1992, at Joe Pool Lake, two little girls saw Her standing in the sky. At the time they were perhaps six and seven years old. They have since grown into lovely young ladies. That was the first year the sun spun and pulsed. The miracle of the sun has been seen by many, including skeptics, and non-believers. But then each year believers have not seen a thing either, so what makes one person "see" and another not, I don't have a clue. Since that first year Mother Mary has also been in other places with people who gathered in their areas at the time of the apparition.*

*When the little girls began to describe Mother Mary as beautiful, I prayed to be able to see her face. The next year, 1993, again there were about one hundred people present. We were looking at the sunset when Byron came over to me to ask if I could see the "face in the clouds." As hard as I tried I could not detect a face in the clouds. He pointed and pointed and I still couldn't see anything. Our friend, Sally, had distanced herself from the group and walked up a small rise. She had a clear view and says that she was so mesmerized that she forgot she had a camera in her hands, until the face began to crunch together. She took a picture of it, and it's on the back cover of the book* Mary's Message of Hope, Vol. 1.

*One other interesting story about the face in the clouds is that my good friends Anita and Roger had gone to Austin, Texas, that weekend and were on their way back to Dallas. They saw the face in the clouds and from 150 miles away. It was a very large face and at the beginning; I'm told, it was so distinct you could see eyelashes and Her hairline. I had to wait to see the picture. Several other people saw it. I saw Her that year as I do every year as the standing Madonna.*

*There have been many other ways I've seen her. One year I saw the standing Madonna briefly, and then a huge, brilliant blue ball filled the upper half of the sky. It was a royal blue color that is seen in neon signs, but it shimmered with different tones. I sat and looked at it thinking, what is this? Then I heard Her. She said, "This is me in my true essence, beyond shape, or form, or any other earthly identity." To me it indicated that in our real identity we are balls of light—when we can go past all these earthly considerations.*

*Lately She has been asking me to identify with my spirit and not with my body, or persona. I often think of that ball of brilliant, shimmering blue light. She is beautiful, with or without shape or form. She gives substance to the word tolerance. She has been most patient, kind, gentle, and loving in all Her interactions with me. I feel that I'm one of Her problem children, because I don't have the awe, or whatever it is, that many of my Catholic friends have. To me she is the loving mother, who loves beyond human comprehension of love, tolerance, understanding, or patience.*

*This year I was talking with Barbara, from California, about Mother Mary. Barbara, who is Catholic, cringed when I related some of my interactions with Mother Mary. Often people react that way. But Mother Mary has never made me feel less than, or lacking, in my way of relating to Her. She fully sees into my heart and knows that although I've never been Catholic, and don't relate to Her in the way my Catholic friends do, I love Her.*

*My experiences have been many and deeply moving. Because of my association and work with Mother Mary, I've changed. She has been my biggest supporter, but has not waved a magic wand my way. I'm told that I must live this life to the best of my ability, in my own way—remembering that the most important command-*

*ment that Christ gave was to love God above all else, and to love our neighbor as ourself. I love Her and know that some day I will see Her when this life ends, and the rest of my life continues. I pray you have a wonderful fall. —annie*

⋄ ⋄ ⋄

My Dear Children, I come to you with hope in my heart for you. Many of you are despairing as you find yourselves in different circumstances. It doesn't matter the cause of the circumstances, for one set of problems is equal to another. It's in how you cope, how you face them, that makes the difference. When you are "in the problem," it feels insurmountable at times and can make you feel overwhelmed. It may be a struggle to live through trying times, and at best can be taxing. Today I bring you hope.

Remember that no matter what the problem entails, it can be completely eradicated or lessened to a great degree, if you solve it from the inside out. All your earthly problems have a beginning inside of you. There is an underlying cause to all problems and issues, and when you tackle the underlying cause, it can be healed, dissolved, and forgiven. This is true with all problems. You may be struggling with an addiction or abuse. It could be a health crisis, financial issues, divorce, death, loss, mental or emotional issues. All problems and issues are solvable or ameliorated through a correcting of your inner life.

This world is the place to express your inner strength, your inner power, and your inner connection to God. This is a world of expression. It was created for you to live according to God's will. It is a world of choice, because God made it so. It is your choice to do God's will or not. It is your choice to live in peace or not. It is your choice to be happy or not. It is your choice to love or hate. It is your choice to be tolerant or rigid. It is your choice to be understanding or unfeeling. It is your choice to be compassionate or merciful. And it is your choice to face your issues or not.

All things can be faced, resolved, and forgiven with hope. Hope, my children, gives you the expectancy of good. Hope can fill your mind and heart with trust. When you have hope in your heart, you can rely on God to bring good into all situations. There are no hopeless situations when you face them with God's help. God has already filled you with His attributes. You have the strength deep inside you to face all manner of things: addictions, abuse, intolerance, fear, terror, rage, injustice, betrayal, even death. Hope is the essence that I wish you to harbor in your hearts and minds. It is important that you hold on to hope.

Hope will give you the faith to face the tough issues of life. Hope will give you the outlook of goodness and resolution. When you expect things to go well, they usually do. When you expect to have strength, it is called up from the depths of you. Hope opens the inner doors to the strength, the courage, the valor, that you need in order to change your life. It is much easier to change the outside of you than the inside. It is easy to buy new clothes, to change your outer appearance by changing hair style, body size, and muscle tone. But dear ones, these things do not change the real you. You can eat all the fashionable diets, adhere to new ways of acting, but these do not change the inner you. It is not the outer diet that I would have you cater to, but to the diet of your thoughts, of feelings.

Do you watch what you wear and neglect what you think? Do you eat what is today considered healthy and ignore what you are feeling? If your heart is filled with fear, with self-hate, with self-centeredness, then you are looking to change that which does not affect your spirit and soul. If you stay in despair and depression, you ignore the beauty of your soul. If you harbor hateful thoughts towards anyone, or anything, then you add to the violence that is in the world. If you refuse to forgive because of pride, you add to the injustices of the world. What you do in your own little area affects greatly what happens to everyone in the world.

The more hope you can maintain, the more the world moves towards peace. For hope is the expectation of good. Hope is the reliance on goodness which is God. Hope is the belief in a higher purpose and just outcome for all situations and circumstances. Hope hungers for a better resolution to situations and circumstances. No matter how good it is, it is wise to keep hope alive in your heart at all times. You may think, I don't need to be concerned with hope, because my life is good. But you do need to keep hope alive—if not for you, do it for the people who are enslaved in addictions, prisons, tyranny, and in abusive circumstances not of their doing.

The more we hold hope in our hearts and minds, the quicker we move into peace. Hope anticipates the best outcome. Hope helps you maintain a cheerful outlook in the face of disaster. Hope says all things are working towards good, because I believe in a loving God. Hope encourages you to be faithful. These are some of the reasons that I ask you to be hopeful at all times, in all circumstances and situations. The more you maintain hope for the goodness of all world situations, the quicker we move towards peace.

As you keep hopeful for world circumstances, you help raise the consciousness of man. You help people from all parts of the world to take a look at what is going on in their part of the world with truth. You change the outcome of world situations more than any war can. You change it with your prayers, your meditations, and your hopes. This is still a time of transition. It is a time for change, but to anticipate that the changes will bring disaster is to lose hope. No matter how the changes occur, it is up to you to stay hopeful. You are to be hopeful that every situation will work out to be good, that circumstances will always be good in the end.

When you are hopeful, you look beyond appearances. Where there is war, hope sees peace. Where there is hatred and prejudices, hope sees tolerance and compassion. Where there is addiction, hope sees healing. Where there is abuse, hope sees forgiveness. Where there is fear, hope sees love. Where there is violence, hope sees serenity. This is my charge to you. Hope and anticipate the best possible outcome to bad situations. Hope and trust in the goodness of God. Hope and desire for all people to have the assurance that God loves them more than anyone can fathom. He does! He loves each person unconditionally and without limit. His love is your peace, your trust, your power, and your hope. Remember this always.

Mary, Mother of Jesus.

# Messages to Our Family

*From the Brotherhood, Mother Mary, and Jesus*

ANNIE AND BYRON KIRKWOOD

ISBN: 0-931892-81-3, 432 pp., $24.95

*"Gather your family together to pray and meditate,"* they requested.

Originally conveyed over five years to Annie and Byron for their weekly family gatherings, this most powerful, beautiful, and thorough course conveys life-changing lessons in spirituality. In the most loving and inspiring manner, the family group was taught how to pray and meditate, to turn within, ask for help, and learn to grow in unconditional love.

# Instructions for the Soul

*Prayers, Affirmations, and Meditations for Daily Living*

ANNIE AND BYRON KIRKWOOD

ISBN: 0-931892-34-1, 192 pp., $12.95

At the request of many people whose lives have been touched by *Messages to Our Family*, a shorter version has been compiled that focuses on prayer and meditation—how to pray, the reasons for praying, the format for and power of group prayer, and how to meditate.

Available from

**Blue Dolphin Publishing, Inc.**

FINE BOOKS FOR ALL AGES

**Orders: 1-800-643-0765 • FAX (530) 477-8342**

# Mary's Message of Hope, Vol. 1

*As Sent to Her Messenger*

ANNIE KIRKWOOD

ISBN: 0-931892-35-X, 168 pp., $12.95

*"Dear children, pray without ceasing. Do this always, sending thoughts of love and hope to all people of the world."*

Mother Mary urged Annie to begin a bi-monthly newsletter to keep in touch with all Her readers. *Mary's Message of Hope, Volume 1* collects the messages given by Mother Mary in the *Newsletter* from April 1992 to October 1996.

*"Mary's inspiring, yet practical, messages touch my heart and my mind and wrap themselves around me in tenderness. Thank you, Annie, for being a much-needed messenger to those who seek spiritual understanding and growth in this lifetime."*
 —Jean K. Foster, writer of *The God-Mind Connection*

### Survival Guide for the New Millennium
*How to Survive the Coming Earth Changes*
BYRON KIRKWOOD

ISBN: 0-931892-54-6, 112 pp., $9.95

Inspired by *Mary's Message to the World*, this is a practical guide to preparing for and surviving natural emergencies.

Available from
**Blue Dolphin Publishing, Inc.**
FINE BOOKS FOR ALL AGES
Orders: 1-800-643-0765 • FAX (530) 477-8342

MORE MESSAGES FROM MARY

# Mary's Message of Love

*As Sent by Mary, the Mother of Jesus, to Her Messensger*

ANNIE KIRKWOOD

ISBN: 0-931892-33-3, 152 pp., $14.95

*"God cannot work for you; He can only work through you."*
—Annie Kirkwood

In the first half of *Mary's Message of Love,* Annie Kirkwood gives specific examples of how she and family members used all the aspects of forgiveness and unconditional love to heal issues involving drug addiction, phobias, physical disabilities, birth defects, panic attacks, and childhood abuse

After Mother Mary urged Annie to write about this topic, she started supplying new messages about unconditional love. The second half of the book is to you from Her. She gives specific examples of what love is and is not. In her ever gentle and loving way, Mary urges us to find heaven within by devoting time every day to meditation and prayer. She urges us to love God by recognizing Him in ourselves and in every person.

Available from
**Blue Dolphin Publishing, Inc.**
FINE BOOKS FOR ALL AGES
Orders: 1-800-643-0765 • FAX (530) 477-8342

*"This book has great impact."* —Marianne Williamson

# Mary's Message to the World

*As sent by Mary, Mother of Jesus, to Her Messenger,* ANNIE KIRKWOOD

ISBN: 0-931892-66-X, 228 pp., paper, $14.95

**This eloquent and inspiring book of messages from the Virgin Mary speaks to all of us about the power of love, truth and prayer.**

In 1987, an extraordinary thing happened to Annie Kirkwood. In her mind, this retired nurse began to sense the presence of the Virgin Mary, entrusting to her messages of vital importance. Mary said that she had chosen Annie deliberately, as a sincere seeker of spiritual truth who could be trusted to transmit her teachings in plain language to ordinary people.

**Mary's Message to the World**
*available on CD:* **$49.95**
The unabridged text of the book compiled from a series of "talks" given by Mary, the Mother of Jesus, from 1987 to 1991.

Reading by Claire Applegate and Matthew Carlton. Includes music, "Mary's Lullaby" by Claire Applegate.

Available from
**Blue Dolphin Publishing, Inc.**
FINE BOOKS FOR ALL AGES
**Orders: 1-800-643-0765 • FAX (530) 477-8342**

www.ingramcontent.com/pod-product-compliance
Lightning Source LLC
Chambersburg PA
CBHW030324080526
44584CB00012B/696